D0585437

Best Wishes

FAROKH ENGINEER

FROM THE FAR PAVILION

FAROKH ENGINEER

FROM THE FAR PAVILION

JOHN CANTRELL

FOREWORD BY JOHN MAJOR

TEMPUS

In loving memory of my parents, Minnie and Manecksha, together with my brother
Darius, to whom I owe everything, with deepest affection and gratitude.

Farokh Engineer

First published 2004

Tempus Publishing Ltd
The Mill, Brimscombe Port
Stroud, Gloucestershire GL5 2QG

© John Cantrell, 2004

The right of John Cantrell to be identified as the Author
of this work has been asserted in accordance with the
Copyrights, Designs and Patents Act 1988.

British Library Cataloguing in Publication Data.
A catalogue record for this book is available from the British Library.

ISBN 0 7524 2736 9

Typesetting and origination by Tempus Publishing.
Printed in Great Britain by Midway Colour Print, Wiltshire.

Contents

Acknowledgements

The authors would like to thank Revd Malcolm Lorimer and Keith Hayhurst of Lancashire County Cricket Club, Ravindra Kumar, the Director and Managing Editor of *The Statesman*, The Rt Hon. John Major CH for writing the foreword, Mihir Bose for the invaluable information contained in his *A History of Indian Cricket*, John Bever for his meticulous proof reading and Julie and Sarah for their unflinching support and encouragement throughout this project. Wherever possible, memory has been checked against the record, for which purpose thanks are due to Wisden and CricInfo.

Foreword

Farokh Engineer is one of the great entertainers of cricket. Whether behind the stumps or with a bat in his hand, he commands both the attention and the enjoyment of his audience. He is the same off the field – buoyant and a bundle of fun, anxious to enjoy life to the full.

Farokh lives his life as if there is no tomorrow and as much as possible must therefore be crammed into today. Caution and 'percentage' batting are alien concepts to this buccaneer, although frustration with an injudicious shot that cuts short his batting is a familiar sensation to those who have followed his career.

As a wicketkeeper, Farokh is among the best I have ever seen: unconventional sometimes, but with astonishing reflexes as the impossible catch or stumping is made to seem commonplace.

Cricket is rich in characters – more so, I think, than in any other sport – and Farokh Engineer can take his proper place in the pantheon of them.

The Rt Hon. John Major CH
September 2002

Introduction

Farokh Engineer retired from professional cricket in 1976. In the quarter century or so since this event he has considered writing his memoirs or an autobiography on a number of occasions – indeed he often refers to a lost manuscript – but the completion of such a task has always eluded him as business affairs and family commitments have taken precedence. To date he is surely one of the few distinguished cricketers of his generation to have remained virtually silent in print. This is all the more surprising when one considers his swashbuckling and colourful personality, a past full of incident and a boyhood craze for reading the lives of great cricketers. My own friendship with Farokh is a recent affair, dating only from the beginning of 2001. We met at the Manchester Bridge Club. Halfway through an evening's session, Farokh joined my table and introduced himself. It took a few seconds for the name to sink in but when the penny finally dropped I couldn't help myself from remarking, 'But you're a famous cricketer'. Farokh later told me in jest that his confidence in my judgement was rooted in that moment. From that time onwards we began to play bridge together as partners (Farokh's card playing was just as flamboyant, spontaneous and full of risk-taking as his batting) and I got round to asking him whether he had ever told his life story. It was a short step from this conversation to offering my services as biographer.

We would meet at regular intervals at his home, appropriately named 'The Far Pavilion' in Mere, Cheshire, where I was always given a warm welcome by his wife Julie, and daughters Roxanne and Scarlett. I would be armed with an antiquated reel-to-reel tape recorder and microphone while Farokh plied me with beers, curries and anecdotes. The results of those meetings form the backbone of this book. In a sense, what follows is a departure from the critical objectivity of conventional biography. This is not a 'warts and all' study. It is, rather, a belated celebration of Farokh's life and cricketing achievements. Wherever possible I have let him tell the story in his own words, which are reproduced verbatim on the page. I have intervened to provide introductory sections and links between Farokh's words and also to acknowledge his successes in a way that only an outsider can do if the subject's modesty is to be preserved. My role has therefore been a combination of biographer, editor, advocate and admirer.

To seasoned cricket enthusiasts Farokh Engineer needs little introduction. But for the benefit of the very young, forgetful or unversed, a few summary words of assessment are perhaps appropriate. Sir Donald Bradman considered Farokh 'one of the world's great wicket-keeper batsmen', and Sir Leonard Hutton's verdict was that 'he must certainly be classed as one of the best wicket keeper batsmen of all time'. Tom Graveney wrote:

> Farokh 'Rooky' Engineer is one of the greatest wicket-keepers India has produced. He was acrobatic and had tremendously fast reflexes, getting to the ball and removing the bails in a flash if the batsman's foot was raised. Farokh was also a top-flight batsman and served both India and Lancashire with distinction.

These twin talents enabled Farokh to play a key role in the transition of India from what might be considered a second division side, alongside New Zealand and Pakistan, to one of first-rank international status and an equally important part in the renaissance of Lancashire County Cricket after the lean years of the 1950s and 1960s. The former contribution was acknowledged by Don Mosey of the BBC:

> Farokh Engineer has probably done more than any other player to promote Indian cricket to world class status – certainly he has done more than any player since the war, in a period when Indian cricket was emerging as something more than endurance-test batting and high-quality spin bowling.

Ray Illingworth wrote in similar vein when he claimed that 'India's emergence as a world class side probably owed more to Farokh than any member of the side, including their World Class spin bowlers'. When Farokh joined Lancashire in 1968 the county had not won a major honour since 1950. Eight years later they had won the Gillette Cup four times and the John Player League twice. But Farokh's contribution to the game of cricket goes beyond his batting averages and work behind the stumps. He was one of the great characters of the game, infecting all with his good humour, selflessness and zest for life. Colin Cowdrey clearly recognised these qualities:

> In all my cricket years, and I mean this most sincerely, I have not known anyone who has embodied the true spirit of cricket more completely than Farokh Engineer. He is the keenest and liveliest of cricketers.

John Arlott wrote: 'His cricket is spontaneous; he plays it as he does because it is his nature to enjoy the game, and he sees no reason to conceal that enjoyment.'

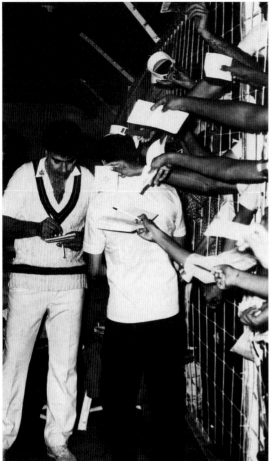

Hot property.

Farokh was both an entertaining and exciting player, an instant hit with the young and an excellent ambassador for the game. Sometimes dubbed 'the gay cavalier' (his other nicknames included the 'Persian Pirate' and the 'Pied Piper of Cricket'), his essential message was that cricket was to be played and enjoyed to the full. He has been compared by Eric Todd of *The Guardian* to a cricketing version of Don Quixote: 'always looking for some new adventure, always prepared, so to say, to tilt at windmills whenever he opens the batting.' Derek Hodgson of the *Daily Express* noted that while Farokh 'could drive with the best', he could also 'use his bat like a two-handed longsword'. It was this unpredictable, exuberant and vital approach to almost everything Farokh attempted in cricket that made him such a favourite with the crowds. There was, of course, a reverse side to these talents, for if Farokh could dazzle and inspire with breathtaking shots, he could also frustrate and dismay, sometimes losing his wicket to reckless and impatient strokes. Yet, as Neville Cardus once remarked, it is almost impossible to combine brilliance with consistency.

Above: The Pied Piper of Cricket.

Right: The two-handed longsword.

Farokh was a cricketing meteor, a shooting star, sparkling, refreshing and exotic. At times his tenure of the crease was tantalisingly short but some would argue that this was the price of his genius.

Farokh Engineer remains a popular figure, especially in India where he is still recognised and mobbed on the streets. He receives about half a dozen postal requests for autographs each week and was recently nominated amongst the top 100 of the best-looking Asian males of the twentieth century by *Indiatimes*. In England he is regularly invited to sporting functions, to after-dinner speaking engagements and other events ranging from the judging of beauty contests to fund-raising ventures for underprivileged and terminally ill children. His cricketing reputation has undoubtedly assisted his business activities which, in turn, have enabled him to live comfortably amongst the sporting élite of north Cheshire. Farokh's philosophy 'always to go for it' has ensured that if he ever failed to achieve an objective it was not for the want of trying. His life is one of attacking enthusiasm, of saying yes rather than no and preferring to take a chance than opt for safe and pedestrian ways. At the age of sixty-five he is still a bundle of energy, still working to improve his business affairs, still encouraging and provoking the young. This is the tale of a man who looks forward to the future as much as he reflects on the past.

Above: Well positioned at fine leg.

Left: Sometimes compared to Englebert Humperdinck – but only with his mouth shut.

one

Family Matters

Farokh Engineer is from India, yet his surname is decidedly English. Despite an educated middle-class background and a natural curiosity about the world, he knows little about his immediate forebears. Yet it seems likely that sometime in the nineteenth century his great-great-grandfather was employed in the newly formed engineering industry, perhaps working on the railways or in the dockyards or government-controlled powder mills. Hence, like many of the English, Farokh sports an occupationally-related surname. Farokh is a name of Persian extraction meaning joy or brightness. Significantly it was at the moment when the lights were turned on for the evening in the Bombay hospital of Farokh's birth that he first entered the world. If Farokh's immediate past is shrouded in uncertainty, the history of his more distant ancestors is much clearer. For Farokh is a Parsee and the Parsees were originally from Persia, the modern-day Iran. Moslem persecution between the eighth and tenth centuries forced them to leave their homeland, still nursing the flames from their sacred fire, and seek refuge abroad in sail boats. Many found sanctuary in western India, especially around Bombay. The local ruler allowed them to maintain their own customs and traditions such that they always retained a sense of separateness from the indigenous population – 'the Jews of India', as they have sometimes been called. When India was colonised by the British the Parsees proved willing collaborators and even today a large number of Parsee households are adorned with portraits of the royal family. Many Parsees became traders, businessmen and members of the professions.

When Farokh was born on 25 February 1938 India was still a British colony, although various concessions had been made to self-government. One of the most obvious signs of India's colonial status was the prevalence of cricket throughout the subcontinent. In one sense the game was a symbol of British rule, yet the Indian population was always able to distinguish between the intrinsic merits of the game and those who had introduced it to their country. Playing cricket was not regarded as a demonstration of support for the Raj or

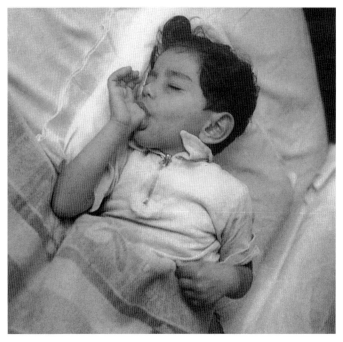

Dreaming of Test cricket.

a symbol of the white man's domination. The Engineer family was typical of many Indian families who watched or played cricket because it combined intelligence with skill, fitness and athleticism and provided gladiatorial encounters without bloodshed. It was an essentially civilized sport, sometimes demanding great patience, in which fate also played a significant role with what could be decisive tosses of the coin and changing pitch and weather conditions. It naturally appealed to a gentle, civilized people who had not always been able to control their own destiny.

During his early years Farokh enjoyed the security of a thoroughly supportive family, the immediate core of which was his father, mother and older brother. These three key figures were the most important formative influences on the new arrival in the family. Farokh's father Manecksha was a medical doctor – Dr Engineer, as he liked to joke. He worked as a general practitioner for TATA, the giant industrial conglomerate which had fingers in virtually every pie from airlines to chemicals and paper manufacture. In 1938 he was based in Bombay and living in Dadar, a prosperous suburb which has been compared to Pudsey in Yorkshire – but only in regard to the number of Test cricketers it has produced (Tamhane, Gupte, Desai, Gavaskar and Tendulkar all grew up in or close to Dadar). Shortly afterwards Dr Engineer was posted to Bhivpuri, a pretty village settlement in the mountains some 100 miles from Bombay where TATA were building a dam to service the needs of a power station. The village was surrounded by thick jungle where maneaters – leopards, panthers and tigers – and other dangerous beasts, including

Minnie and Manecksha.

elephants, would prowl and claim the occasional life or limb of a hapless villager or part of their herd of cattle. On such occasions Dr Engineer would be summoned, for he was the only local equipped with a rifle. If the young Farokh went with him on these dangerous missions he would be told to climb up the tallest tree 'and not breathe a word' until the threat was seen off or killed. Dr Engineer was a tall, bespectacled, well-built man, respected and admired by all who knew him but especially by his youngest son:

He was an extremely mild-mannered, extremely polite person. In fact, I've never – and I mean that, never – seen my dad lose his temper. He never said one wrong word about anyone and he was just too good to be true. He was a marvellous doctor; people that didn't even know him used to ring him in the middle of the night and he used to take his medical kit and go. If ever there was an honour I think my dad should have got it because he really served the community and we were in a village where there were no doctors at all for hundreds of miles, literally. Dad had to perform the trickiest operations because he was the only one with medical knowledge and saved so many lives there – people were bitten by poisonous snakes and all sorts. Operations, he had to do them – it was him or the butcher, and my dad had to perform these operations or the people would have died. He was a voracious reader; he was up to date with medical books all the time. He was an extremely intelligent person and he just loved sport: he was a very good tennis player and a very good cricketer, at club standard. He had a very dry

15

sense of humour, not too blasé, a very soft-spoken, mild-mannered man. Gosh, I'm extremely the opposite!

Many of the stories about Manecksha Engineer reveal a man equally devoted to his son, a man willing to sacrifice, foster and encourage in every conceivable way in order to promote the skills of an emerging talent:

He was an opening bowler and used to be pretty useful with a new ball. He used to come and bowl to me sometimes. He started off bowling slowly but gradually got faster as I started hitting him to all corners of the ground. Sometimes, when there was no-one to practise with, Dad used to come and bowl to me and (there were no fielders) I used to hit the ball over his head or wherever and, poor chap, he used to run miles and get it and bowl the next ball and I used to hit it again. Now I feel so bad making dad do all the running, but he just wanted me to be a good player.

Manecksha sometimes found it impossible to conceal his pride and interest, even at the risk of earning a filial rebuke:

My Dad used to love coming to watch me play and I used to feel extremely embarrassed because no-one else's father would come to watch. I used to plead with him, 'Please don't come, I can't concentrate,' and he promised that he wouldn't come. But he was so, so keen and I never forget one day it was raining, it was an ordinary club match and we carried on playing in the light drizzle. Someone mentioned, 'Farokh, your father is getting wet.' He was standing under a tree, virtually hiding. 'Please ask him to come and sit in the pavilion, we would love to welcome him there.' That's when I realised my Dad was there and when that person told me I felt so bad and I signalled to my Dad and he was so pleased.

In contrast to the rather quiet, easygoing and unassuming father, Farokh's mother, Minnie, had something of the extrovert about her. The daughter of a doctor, she too was a keen sportswoman, an excellent tennis player and an avid follower of her son's cricketing successes – but via the radio commentaries. When Farokh arrived home after a game she would ask him, 'Why did you get out to that ball?' It was always a source of regret to Farokh that she never lived to see him become famous in terms of making an impact in international cricket. Farokh describes her as 'a great lady' and adds that he 'still worships her and thinks of her every day'. In addition to sport, Minnie played the piano and violin and Farokh describes her as 'culturally refined'. Indeed she came from a musical family which included the conductor Zubin Mehta, who held appointments as Musical Director of the New York Philharmonic Orchestra, the Israel Philharmonic Orchestra and Bavarian State Opera Orchestra. He is popularly associated with the Three Tenors and

Farokh's mother, Minnie.

conducted their concerts in Rome and Los Angeles. Zubin used to come and watch Farokh play Test cricket:

He used to be in the player's enclosure as my guest and these young kids came running up to me for autographs and I'm signing away merrily there. One little lad asked for Zubin's autograph and Zubin said, 'Why do you want my autograph?' 'Because you are Farokh Engineer's cousin,' came the reply. Over the years Zubin and I have had a chuckle over this and he often used to tease me by asking, 'And how's my famous cousin?'

Minnie's sense of natural justice, even embracing the animal kingdom, is illustrated by the story of the cobra, an event which took place when Farokh was about three or four years of age:

Mum used to place me on the lawn with my toys while she used to do her work. She left me for just a few minutes but when she got back a huge cobra was right by my side and he was shaking his neck one way and the other and I was virtually playing with him shaking my own neck from side to side. It seemed as if he was copying me! These are the most venomous killers, but he must have seen me as a child and not going to do him any harm. As soon as my Mum and the servants saw what was happening they panicked because the cobra was within striking distance of me, about a foot. But all of a sudden, the cobra put his head down, turned round and very slowly moved towards the tall grass. The servants ran out with sticks to try and kill him but my Mum stopped them. She said, 'Don't hurt him, he hasn't hurt my son.'

Minnie was as keen as Manecksha that the young Farokh should excel at his sport, but she was determined that his academic studies should not suffer. Lessons and homework had to take precedence over cricket practice, and the diminutive Minnie would climb onto a chair so that she could wedge a stopper between the door and the door frame to prevent her son from escaping. The stopper would only be removed when the schoolwork was complete. There was one occasion on the eve of a set of examinations when the secretary of the local cricket club, keenly aware of the matriarchal house rules, crept up to the Engineer family home in order to persuade Farokh to play in an important game. Minnie had gone out, so thinking that he could complete his revision in the evening, Farokh collected his bat, pads and gloves and set off for the match:

I was batting and scoring runs when I saw my mum walk onto the pitch and march all the way to where I was standing. 'You… Out,' she shouted, 'You're coming home now, you haven't done your lessons.' And she took me off the field in the middle of a club game telling off the other players: 'Would you allow your sons to play a cricket match the day before his exams? He has all the time in the world afterwards but he has to pass his exam.' I was so annoyed with her and so embarrassed but eventually I passed my exam and had to thank her for it.

Minnie was health conscious, keeping buffalo for milk instead of cows. From a medical family and married to a doctor, Minnie had little time for high-tech medicine and relied instead on home-spun remedies:

Mum was a great believer in honey, pure honey. We used to get our servants to collect pure honey from the mountains and whenever myself or my brother was ill, or anyone else, mum gave us a teaspoon of honey. And Dad was suggesting antibiotics and all sorts of things but she said, 'leave all that rubbish alone, just have my honey and you will be all right,' and by golly she was right. Honey never did us any harm and we were as right as rain the next day.

Minnie's whole life was devoted to the welfare of her children. This was even apparent at meal times:

Mother and son.

When we had a roast or lobster or whatever my brother Darius used to have the best piece and I used to have the second best piece. If we had a fish, for example, Darius used to have the best, I the second best, Dad used to have the third best and Mum would finish with the head, literally. Not literally the head, but near. She was a very self-sacrificing lady and she enjoyed doing that because she just wanted the best for her children.

Although assisted by servants, Minnie did most of the cooking and the shopping. Young Farokh would often accompany her to the fish market:

She used to press the fish in the right spot to find if the fish was fresh or not. Those things were taken for granted in the fish markets of Bombay. You can't go into Marks & Spencer today and start squeezing the fish; that wouldn't make you very popular.

But despite Minnie's insistence on natural remedies, a good wholesome diet (avoiding chillies and vinegar) and physical fitness, she died relatively young and quite suddenly in her early fifties. Farokh was some 500 miles away from Bombay playing cricket at Jamnagar when Minnie was taken into hospital:

I got a message that my Mum had been taken ill and would I return home. My family had never interrupted me from a cricket match before so I knew that something was very, very serious. The last flight to Bombay was at 3 p.m. and it was already 3.15 p.m. by the time I got the message. The nearest airport was at a place called Ahmedabad 300 miles drive away. Jamnagar was a state run by a Maharaja; they were all very keen on cricket, cricketers stayed at their palaces and were entertained lavishly. He gave a load of rupees to his old driver who drove a huge Cadillac, left-hand drive and one of the old models. The Maharaja said, 'Just take Farokh to Bombay or to Ahmedabad and try to catch the plane. I will phone Indian Airlines to see if they will hold onto the plane.' This driver drove the car at 30mph on the dirt-track roads. I calculated the time very quickly and realised that we wouldn't reach anywhere in six hours at this speed. So I told the driver to come into my seat and I took the controls. I had never driven a left-hand drive car in my life before and I was tearing, I must have been going at about 100mph to catch that flight and we were about half an hour late. Indian Airlines had held onto the plane but the flight was full and passengers were told that Farokh Engineer's mother was ill and Farokh needed a seat on the plane (I was just beginning to gain a reputation at this stage). Would you believe that each and every passenger said I could have their seat and in the end the captain said, 'There is no need for that. He can come in the jump seat.' The captain told me about this during the flight and I went out and thanked everyone over the speaker system. Anyway I landed and dashed to the hospital, arriving between eight and ten o'clock in the evening. I was at Mum's bedside all through the night with tears streaming down my face because I knew she was dying and the doctors had said she was fading away. Suddenly my Mum put her hand on my head and said, 'Don't cry son, I promise I will come back to you as your first daughter.' Those were the only words she spoke to me and with her hand on my head she passed away. And I knew that my first child was going to be a girl.

The cause of Minnie's death was never established and she died while under medical observation. Her husband lived another twenty years on his own, surviving cancer of the throat, until he succumbed to old age in his early nineties.

Minnie and Manecksha were both Parsees and they made sure that their sons were brought up in a way that was consistent with the values of the Parsee religion:

The Parsee religion was not particularly strict, there was nothing rigid saying that you must do this or must not do that. It is said that the Hindus refuse to eat beef while the Moslems refuse pork. The Parsees, however, like their meat medium rare. It was a very simple, very easy religion which stressed three things: good thoughts, good words and good deeds. But I think most religions will tell you that. From time to time we would visit the Fire Temple where the flame is never allowed to go out. It was transported across the Arabian Sea from Persia centuries ago; every fire temple in the world burns a flame from this same source. Outside the temple we would buy some sandalwood to put on the fire, creating a sweet-smelling fragrance. My parents never insisted that I go to the temple. They said their prayers at home and tried to promote the virtues of life. We were brought up in a good way. We were not a very religious community though we believed in God and I still say my prayers every night before going to bed, thanking my parents and my prophet Zarathustra for all they have done for me.

The Parsees lived in a very westernised way and came into close contact with the British, imitating many of their customs and traditions, such as a good English breakfast with bacon, eggs and mushrooms. In fact, just about everything except black pudding! We would celebrate Christmas, Diwali [the Hindu New Year], *Id* [the Moslem New Year] *and Nowroz, the Parsee New Year, exchanging cards and presents. On the whole the Parsees were an affluent community, including top industrialists such as the Tata family, top lawyers, surgeons and educationalists. They built hospitals, schools and libraries and generally did a lot for the Indian community. Of course, because they were successful there was some jealousy and fun would be poked at the old-fashioned Parsee in just about every Indian movie; there he would be with certain exaggerated mannerisms which even I would laugh at. My only criticism of the religion is that it is too exclusive. Other religions try to spread their gospel and recruit new members, but not so the Parsees. Even my wife Julie, who is English, is prevented from becoming a Parsee because she wasn't born one. It is exceedingly snobbish and, regrettably, a dying religion because no new members are admitted. The leading elders could surely take steps to make people more aware of this beautiful religion and change certain principles especially with regard to the membership.*

One of my strongest memories concerning the religion involves birthdays and weddings. On birthdays we used to dress up in new white shirts and shorts or trousers before visiting the Fire Temple, while for weddings there would be a feast with the tastiest food in the world. The celebrations would include a 'nankhatai' band which nearly always played out of tune, but with great gusto, and the food would be served on banana leaves. It was fantastic. There was nothing to beat that banquet.

The third pivotal figure in Farokh's childhood was his brother Darius, five and a half years his senior. Darius was also a keen sportsman and according to Farokh 'was a far better cricketer than I ever was but he never played Test cricket'. The reason for this was apparently 'politics in Indian cricket' for he was 'a brilliant off-spinner and attacking batsman'. It was Darius who encouraged his younger brother to take up wicketkeeping:

He was a terrific off-spinner and could turn the ball square on any track. For the club side wicketkeepers, leg-side ball-gathering was something unheard of then. Every time the ball turned it was just four byes. Darius used to get frustrated and one day the regular wicketkeeper was absent and the only way I could get in the team was by keeping wicket to take his place. My

Brother Darius.

brother came on to bowl his off spin and not only was I taking the balls down leg side but I had a couple of leg-side stumpings which was completely unheard of. Leg-side stumpings! How can you stump a batsman when you are blind, it's pure anticipation. And that's what Darius said. 'Gee you should take up wicketkeeping, you'd be absolutely brilliant, you're the best wicketkeeper I've enjoyed bowling to.' Every time we played he insisted that I was the wicketkeeper. And that's how I really got started.

It was also Darius who introduced the young Farokh to the Brabourne Stadium, the scene of so much of his future cricket action with the CCI (the Cricket Club of India and the Indian equivalent of the MCC), with Mumbai and with India. The stadium was built on a piece of land reclaimed from the sea and presented to the CCI by Lord Brabourne, the Governor of Bombay, after he was tempted with the offer of immortality. It was a stadium of contrasts between the luxury of the three-storey stucco pavilion and the segregated wire-caged compounds providing the cheapest seats:

My brother would take me on his shoulders, otherwise I would have been trampled by the crowds in the East Stand. This East Stand made the Stretford End at Old Trafford look like Buckingham Palace. There was only concrete flooring with no seats and you had to stand on this concrete packed like sardines – sardines were much more comfortable in their tins than we were. And we would be over each other's heads and shoulders and everything and

I virtually saw an entire international game perched on my brother's shoulders because it was the only way I could see. I remember Darius taking me to the front row and who should I see having a chewing gum but Denis Compton – he lived in India for a number of years during the war. He was fielding on the boundary line and I must have said, sitting on my brother's shoulders, 'Hello Mr Compton' or 'Hello Denis'. And he just opened a packet of chewing gum and asked if I would like one but I was too nervous to say yes and he just flicked me one, he tossed me one and I caught it. Boy, I didn't eat that chewing gum for years, I think I just kept it and I told Compo about this in later years when we became really good chums in England.

Darius went to England to study structural engineering and design at Imperial College, London. He then began practicing as a structural engineer based in London, but moved to Bowdon, Cheshire, when Farokh began playing for Lancashire. He found it irksome and time-consuming explaining to incredulous customers that both his profession and name were 'Engineer', so he changed his name to Shaw, his father's middle name. Sadly, Darius died in 1997. His name lives on with the Darius Shaw award presented by Farokh each year to the most promising youngster at Mobberley Cricket Club in Cheshire.

In addition to Darius there were also Dossy and Pervin. Minnie was Manecksha's second wife and Dossy and Pervin were the children of the first marriage. Farokh was always a little scared of Dossy for he was 'pretty strict', but he still enjoyed his company because Dossy was a mechanic and used to take his half-brother under cars with him while he performed repairs. Better still, Dossy had a motorcycle. Farokh remembers making unauthorised use of this machine on one occasion while his brother was at work. The escapade was originally intended to be a single circuit of the home around the perimeter paving, but this escalated into at least fifteen rounds and then straight out onto the streets to show off to the girls. When Dossy returned he noticed that his motorcycle engine was warm and guessed at what Farokh had been doing but 'didn't seem to mind too much'. Pervin was a God-fearing lady and 'a holy type of person into meditation and all sorts of things'. She lived with her husband, Dhun, in Madras, and Farokh used to take vacations at their home, named 'Cosy Nook'. Here he would sleep on the balcony overlooking the sea. Like Dossy, Dhun also had a motorcycle, which was an obvious attraction for the thrill-seeking Farokh; he even managed to crash it on one occasion.

Other family members make but fleeting appearances in Farokh's recollections of his early years though he has vivid memories of visits to his maternal grandmother who lived in a sixth-floor apartment in Bombay. Farokh remembers sitting on the balcony and throwing ice cubes onto the people below. Such naughtiness would have severely displeased the only other relative to have made a lasting impact, Aunt Nergish, his father's elder sister.

This formidable lady was a headmistress and described by Farokh as both 'a very boisterous old lady' and a 'tyrant'. Her tyranny was primarily exercised on birthdays:

I used to dread my birthdays because when it was my birthday one of the things we had to do was to go and see Nergish aunty and every year I got a bloody pyjama as a birthday present. I never wore pyjamas, I used to always sleep in shorts. She knew I hated bloody pyjamas. And that dreaded kiss. When she used to give us a kiss it was like injections, her lips used to go and scoop up half a gallon of your blood and my brother and I used to dread that kiss from Nergish aunty.

But this was a very minor inconvenience in an otherwise happy childhood. His parents' marriage was undoubtedly successful, with Minnie taking obvious pride in her husband's achievements. Farokh describes the family as 'closely knit and loving' and it clearly provided him with emotional security, a joy of life and the encouragement to pursue his interest in sport to the highest level. Few can demand more of their parents.

two

Backstreets and Beaches

After four or five years living in the jungle settlement of Bhivpuri, the Engineer family returned to their home in Dadar, Bombay. This was a move from a small mountain village to one of the largest and most densely populated cities in the world. Bombay was and is India's principal commercial, financial and industrial centre, with a thriving port on the Arabian Sea and many distinguished educational and cultural institutions. It was also congested, polluted and cursed with some of the largest slum areas on the subcontinent. This was also a move from a spacious bungalow surrounded by well-tended lawns and gardens to the relatively cramped quarters of a city apartment. Property in Bombay is among the most expensive in the world and the Engineers' Dadar home was not large enough for Farokh to enjoy his own room. Indeed there was just one large bedroom furnished with four beds, one for each member of the family. Not surprisingly, Farokh often chose to sleep on the balcony. Here it was much cooler and there was always a good chance of some excitement for he was able to hear when the 'chor, chor' or cry of 'thief' resounded around the local streets. Farokh would join the chase armed with the cricket bat that he always kept by his bedside. There were occasions when the luckless miscreant was caught and would suffer a good beating at the hands of his pursuers. Farokh remembers a number of such victims pleading to be handed over to the police.

Farokh was often assisted in these exploits by his neighbours, the Soonavalla family. There were four brothers – Rusi, Furdoon, Jamshed and Soli – all of whom have since attained positions of eminence within the medical profession. They were a model family, good at sport, excelling in athletics and hockey, and good at their studies. Farokh remembers his own parents regarding the Soonavallas as a benchmark for what should be expected of children. In addition to assisting Farokh trap burglars and prowlers they introduced him to the first steps of dancing on their terrace. Farokh would

Beach cricket in Bombay.

protest that he would never be able to dance but they helped him make progress by suggesting a generous swig of whisky before taking the floor.

It was from this point that Farokh's formal education began. In Bhivpuri lessons were conducted by a private tutor but now, at the age of seven, it was time to go to school. This meant a visit to Eric the Tailor to be fitted up with new shorts and shirts:

He was a dreaded tailor in Bombay, a typical old-fashioned Parsee tradesman, and he just loved pleasing parents. Shorts, I like them a little above the knee, not that I've got golden legs or something, but just a little above the knee. But Eric the Tailor would insist on measuring way below the knee, almost like Bermuda shorts, to please the parents so that if the son grows tall the shorts will last him longer – that was the whole theory that parents don't have to waste more money on clothes. I used to be so annoyed with him, I used to plead, 'please a quarter inch, a quarter inch higher'. Again with shirts, I like my shirts loose but Eric the Tailor used to give you a very loose fit and that too would please the parents. Believe me, it wasn't funny being made to dress up like a Japanese general – especially in one's early teens.

Two years were spent at the Dr Antonio D'Silva School, but Farokh was so playful and indisciplined that Aunt Nergish had her way in persuading her brother to send his youngest son to a boarding school in Poona, the Shri Shivaji Preparatory Military School. Here school life was organised along strict disciplinary lines and the students wore a military uniform. But it was also at the Shivaji school that Farokh learnt his first steps of cricket along with horse riding and swimming. On his return to Bombay the influential Aunt Nergish nearly had a dampening effect on Farokh's cricketing ambitions:

Aunt Nergish said that Farokh was still too naughty and must join the Boy Scouts, so Dad put me in the Boy Scouts and Boy Scouts were on Sunday mornings with a ten o'clock start. That was also the time the cricket matches began on a Sunday and I used to be so disappointed as I was here shouting 'Akela' and all that stuff instead of being in a cricket match. Of course Dad could see my burning desire for cricket and it hurt him to see me so downcast. After a few months he said, 'Forget it, just go back to cricket.' I would have loved to have done the Boy Scouts at some other time but the opportunity never arose.

At the age of eleven Farokh entered another day school located in Dadar, Don Bosco High School. Don Bosco was run by Italian Jesuit priests and was founded in memory of the nineteenth-century Italian-born saint John Bosco, who had once astounded his fellow town dwellers with his acrobatic and juggling skills. Here young Farokh continued his sporting interests playing soccer, becoming the first-team goalkeeper, hockey, squash and badminton. He was also a keen athlete especially at the 100 metres and high jump, at which he claims he could jump more than his own height. But there was no cricket. In fact, Farokh remembers the headmaster, Father McFarlane, trying to discourage him from pursuing his interest in the game:

He would pronounce in a broad Italian accent 'Creecket will not pay you in life son' – and how bloody right he was!

It wasn't until Farokh was almost ready to leave that he persuaded the authorities to allow the school to enter the inter-schools cricket championship. Many years later when Farokh was playing in a Test match at Madras, the headmaster of a local school contacted Farokh at his hotel asking if he was the same Farokh Engineer who had attended the Don Bosco High

School where he had previously been headmaster. Father McFarlane had transferred from Bombay to Madras and now Farokh was famous he invited him to address his new school. Apparently he was so proud that Farokh Engineer was a product of Don Bosco that he promptly saw to it that cricket was made compulsory in all the Don Bosco schools in India.

If Don Bosco did little to launch Farokh into his cricketing career, it provided him with the academic credentials to enter university. His favourite subjects were algebra, geography and French. Farokh was a restless student and the French master, Mr Lobo, once referred to him as 'a monkey on hot bricks'. The mathematics master found him equally troublesome for he was always chatting to his fellow students instead of patiently listening to the instruction:

He had a habit of throwing the wooden duster, wood on one side and felt on the other. He had a pretty good aim. He was writing something on the board and must have heard me talking and threw the duster at me when my eyes were off him. Suddenly someone shouted 'Farokh' and I turned round to see the duster hurtling towards me at 100 miles per hour. Quick as a flash my hand went up and caught it and all the kids in the classroom started laughing. That was the last time he threw the duster at me because he was so worried that I might catch it and embarrass him again.

But while Farokh studied quite hard there was always an element of doubt that he would satisfy the university entrance requirements on account of the time he spent playing cricket out of school. One university professor was determined that his college should not lose such a rich prize:

One of the professors approached me, as he was mad keen on cricket and was trying to build up a college team. This was Podar College of Commerce and Economics. We had to pass an exam called Senior Cambridge/ Matriculation and in my exam I thought I had done reasonably well but you are never sure – have I done well enough in that paper? Will I pass? Will I get enough marks? You are always apprehensive about the result. This professor said that if I would give him my word that I would definitely join his college, they would give me a completely free ship, not having to pay a cent for my education. Plus he wanted me to come and captain the college team and help him build up a cricket team there because he thought that if I joined up other players would follow. He also asked me to give him my exam number so that if, God forbid, I should fail anything he would see that I pass. And I gave my word to this professor but I didn't need his help because I passed – 53% or so. I was quite pleased as I was so busy on the cricket field.

Since Don Bosco provided no facilities for cricket all Farokh's early cricket training and development necessarily took place elsewhere. The Shivaji school had provided some basic instruction, but much of Farokh's cricketing education took place in the open-space playground opposite the Dadar home and on the beaches and backstreets of Bombay, using trees or tin cans as stumps. Farokh claims that he had a ball in his hand almost all the time and remembers a garage wall against which he would spend hours flinging a sponge ball equipped with jagged edges in order to practice his catching skills on the erratic return. His father would also bounce a sponge ball towards him in the family living room, sometimes sacrificing windows and glasses in the cause of his son's cricketing progress. There was a theoretical as well as a practical side to Farokh's early cricketing education, for along with most young Indians he would spend hours memorising 'every Test cricketer's name and every Test cricketer's average' while collecting the miniature signed portraits from petrol stations.

Shortly after returning to Dadar Dr Engineer made his son a member of the Dadar Parsee Colony Sporting Club where Farokh used to go along to watch his brother and father play and snatch the occasional practice in the nets. Soon after this he acquired his first cricket bat:

At first I used a delapidated club bat that was patched up and hardly suitable for firewood. I would use one bat one day and another bat the next, but when I started making some runs and scored my first fifty in about fifteen or twenty minutes or so, somebody said to my father, 'Doctor, you should buy your son a nice cricket bat of his own, he needs to get used to his own bat.' So dad took me to this place, to the sports shop, and I'll never forget the day I bought this cricket bat. But the salesman was trying to palm me off with another branded bat telling me that all the best cricketers used that one. I was a kid and I fancied this other bat as I liked the balance and I got the one I liked in the end. My word, did I put it to good use! It lasted for about three or four years and for a hard-hitting batsman that was really quite something. It was only an Indian bat made out of soft wood because it was the only sort we could afford and we had to patch it up all over the place and there was more sticking plaster on it than wood in the end.

Farokh remembers the occasion when one of his boyhood cricketing heroes, Pahlan (Polly) Umrigar, played at the club:

Polly Umrigar used to make the occasional guest appearance at the Dadar Colony Sporting Club and on one afternoon after he had scored a fifty he came into the pavilion at teatime and asked somebody to bring him a glass of water. Boy, I ran so fast (he didn't even ask me, he asked someone else), I ran like hell, picked up the first glass I could, washed it like I had never washed a glass before, cleaned it and dashed back spilling half the water so I was the first to bring it to him. And he put his hand on my head and said, 'Thank you sonny.' Later on, when we played Test cricket together, I always used to remind him of this incident but he said he couldn't remember it. He was my boyhood hero until I switched my allegiance to Godfrey Evans, which was when I took up wicketkeeping seriously.

Both Polly Umrigar and Godfrey Evans were excellent role models for the young Farokh. Umrigar was twelve years Farokh's senior and was unquestionably one of the all-time greats of Indian cricket. From 1962 to 1978, when he was overtaken by Gavaskar, he held the records for most Tests (59), most runs (3631) and most hundreds (12) scored by an Indian Test player. For thirty years he held the record for getting the highest score by an Indian on tour – 252 not out against Cambridge University in 1959. As a bowler his time of triumph came when he took 4 for 27 against Australia at Kanpur in 1959. He captained India in 8 Tests, was the first Indian to hit a Test double century and in 1962 scored both a century and took 5 wickets in an innings at Port of Spain. Godfrey Evans was, according to Wisden, 'arguably the best wicket keeper the game has ever seen'. His biographer described him as 'a cricketing Falstaff' and energy, enthusiasm and technical excellence were the widely acclaimed hallmarks of his game. He was England's first-choice wicketkeeper between 1946 and 1959, playing in 91 Tests. Evans paid tribute to Farokh by selecting him for the 'Ten Greatest Wicket-Keepers' of all time for a book of cricket lists published in 1984. Like Farokh, Evans was an acrobatic and theatrical performer behind the stumps.

It was at the age of fifteen that Farokh got his first opportunity to play in the team as a result of the absence of the regular wicketkeeper. The story has already been told of how Darius marvelled at his brother's keeping skills, but despite Farokh's impressive debut he was soon dropped from the side when the regular wicketkeeper returned:

I had performed exceedingly well behind the stumps but the competitor guy came back. He was about thirty stones and he was so fat, so huge that they thought the ball is bound to hit him somewhere and he won't give away many byes. But this guy could hardly catch the ball and when they dropped me I could hardly believe it. My father couldn't believe it either and he was so disgusted about the way they had treated me that he resigned from the club. I then joined a rival club, Sassanian Cricket Club, which was some way away from where I lived, about 15 to 20 miles. And both clubs met in the final of this club side competition. Dadar were the champions and were on a hat-trick. I was so determined to do well and my Dad said, 'Boy if you don't get a hundred today... you've got to show them that they've really missed you.' And I got a hundred and the Dadar club really took it to heart, just as dad had predicted. They begged me to come back and play for their club – which I did. They were saying things like, 'How could we have been so blind, so stupid that we didn't pick him.'

With boyhood hero Godfrey Evans.

Farokh played just one season for the Sassanian club before returning to Dadar. At about this time he was made an honorary member of the CCI. Each year the CCI would select two or three promising youngsters to join their trainee or apprenticeship scheme based at the Brabourne Stadium. Although restricted to menial tasks and occasional coaching, Farokh was able to rub shoulders with the cricketing élite and savour the superior quality of the lunches, changing rooms and showers. For the first time Farokh felt in contact with those at the top of the game. It was not to be long before he joined them.

Farokh's preoccupation with cricket still left time for other pursuits such as cycling. On more than one occasion he cycled in a group of some fifteen to twenty friends from Bombay to Poona in the mountains, a round journey of 240 miles through dangerous jungle and forested areas known as the Western Ghats. Leopards and panthers were never far away and the intense heat of the sun meant that an overnight stay was unavoidable. Once a year Farokh would compete in the Don Bosco sportsday cycle race, which entailed ten laps around the school grounds:

This was a most popular race, cheered by everyone in the school. If you won the cycle race you were a hero, the best guy in the school. There was one particular chap who was very keen on cycling but he had a proper racing cycle whereas I had to go on my ordinary bicycle. He had a distinct advantage over me so what I used to do was to go and hire a racing cycle.

But the hire shop was about eight miles away from the school and the hire rental was very expensive. So I used to time it so that I got to the shop, hired the bike, then cycled like mad to the starting point of the race with only minutes to spare and then return the cycle immediately afterwards. I used to be shattered but the hire rental was by the hour and the charge would go up with each extra minute. I won the race on a number of occasions much to the disgust of the fellow with the latest racer with all its gadgets and gears.

There was also time for the cultivation of friendships and the first hesitant, or perhaps not so hesitant, approaches towards members of the opposite sex. Farokh remembers two friends in particular: Sashi Kapoor and Pervez Sinor, not forgetting Vinod Ahuja, the son of a customs officer:

Vinod used to have the best socks. Sashi and I used to have old scruffy socks but this guy used to wear his pants especially high to show off his socks. He was the envy of everyone and his father used to give him all these imported socks with fancy designs and strong colours that they confiscated in the customs house. Such very nice socks.

Sashi went on to become a famous Indian film star working in Bollywood, the Bombay film industry, and married Jennifer, the sister of Felicity Kendal. Pervez was Farokh's closest schoolfriend:

He was very keen on a young lady but he used to wear glasses and most of the girls were after me in those days because I was sporty and playing around and this and that. I was a rogue and girls like rogues, absolute swine I was. I had literally the choice of girls, I could pick anyone I wanted – at least, I used to like to think I could. And this particular girl, we used to walk past her balcony every evening and she lived on the second floor in a flat. Pervez was very self-conscious and used to ask me if I could see her on the balcony because he was so short-sighted he couldn't see. I would say 'yeh yeh' and he would look up and wave and she used to wave back and that would make his evening. The girl's mother was a tyrant, a real battleaxe because she knew all the boys were after her daughter. One day the mother was on the balcony and Pervez asked his usual question. Being playful I said 'yeh yeh' and Pervez gave her a wave. The mother looked daggers and when Pervez realised he ran to hit me, but I could run faster than him and he couldn't catch up.

Farokh clearly enjoyed the social side of his teenage years and the excitement of arranging dates with local girls:

I had quite a few girlfriends from a very young age. I suppose I was a bit of a Romeo and certainly very flamboyant in whatever I did. This seemed to attract female admirers. We would go to the cinema and hang around the

Farokh as a teenager.

streets but there was no sex. Sex was taboo. We just used to have the odd kiss and cuddle but that was it. My mother used to get invitations of marriage for me from other parents and she used to shoo them off – 'My Farokh is only young and he's got a life to lead.' She used to joke about it over the dinner table.

Childhood and adolescence were obviously fun for Farokh. He was good-looking, highly personable and one of the most talented sportsmen about town. It wasn't just cricket that he excelled at, for he played both hockey and squash to almost international level and played soccer to first division standard. These accomplishments developed his self confidence and by his own admission he was 'pretty cocky, almost on the verge of a showman'. He liked to do everything 'with a flair'. But despite the bravado he was also 'exceedingly sensitive'. An unjustified criticism or discourtesy would be taken immediately to heart: 'my feelings could be hurt even by a child very, very quickly, yes indeed.' But most of the time Farokh was living for the moment: lying on his balcony enjoying his favourite Latin American rhythms, spending a lazy day on the beach, cycling in the early morning to the swimming baths, browsing through his stamp collection and thinking of his future. In his early teens Farokh developed the ambition 'of being somebody in life, somebody hopefully in cricket'. He was now on the verge of achieving this ambition.

three

Starlet

The five-year period between 1957 and 1961 saw Farokh's horizons quickly change from being a rising star at the Dadar club to playing Test cricket for India. First it was college cricket. Almost immediately thereafter he was selected for the Bombay University side and the Combined Universities, before being selected for the Indian Starlets who toured Pakistan in 1960. Finally he gained a place in the national squad. This dramatic transition took place during Farokh's university days. He was studying what today would be regarded as a Business Studies degree specialising in advanced accounting and auditing. The course should have lasted four years but Farokh failed a couple of examinations as a result of his cricketing commitments. He had to retake both his intermediate and final examinations so his Bachelor of Commerce eventually took six years to complete.

While at university Farokh was by no means certain that Test cricket was to be his chosen career and he flirted with the idea of becoming a pilot:

When I started at the university we had to join a cadet corps, either Army, Navy or Air Force, and I joined the air-wing. One of the perks was that they taught you to fly and I passed my private pilot's licence at Bombay Flying Club. I had always been fascinated by planes and flying and here I was learning for free. Later on I had an offer from Air India to become a pilot and do extensive training on the jumbos and all that, or I could have joined the Indian Air Force as a fighter pilot in the Fighter Jet Squadron. But mum was strongly opposed to the idea of my having a flying career. She knew that quite a few of the flying cadets had crashed and died, all young boys, and she knew how reckless I was – 'No way are you making flying your career,' she said. So even though there was no professional cricket in India I decided to concentrate on the cricket side of things. There was a lot of glamour attached to the game and if you played international cricket you were really somebody, made for life.

Farokh as an Air Force cadet.

Farokh's youthful recklessness is graphically illustrated by his account of one of his flying antics, a story he prefaces with the remark, 'I don't know how I'm still alive today':

There was a bridge just high enough for a double-decker bus to go through. I used to fly up in a little Piper Cherokee or Tiger Moth or whatever and watch from the sky until I could see that the way was clear and there were no buses approaching the bridge from either side. Then I used to dive down and pass under the bridge, climbing steeply again to avoid crashing into a college building. On the way down I used to go at full speed, literally, right steep as if I was crashing, then pick up the throttle which lifted it up. It was stunt flying, I was a bloody show-off, pure and simple stupidity, trying to impress the girls or whatever. It was just to have a laugh with my mates, they all knew I was this guy for doing something daft like looping the loop and this and that. It was always a single-engine plane and if the engine had failed that would have been game, set and match, but even if the engine had spluttered or sprung an oil leak and the plane had failed to pick up I would have gone straight into a building. (Looking back on these events I can hardly believe the extent of my recklessness which could well have resulted in a major catastrophe – perhaps this fearless attitude paid dividends at a later stage when I was facing some of the fastest bowlers in the world with a minimum of protection.) Each time I did this there were phone calls to the Flying Club about this 'bloody maniac' and I was warned, but luckily my instructor was cricket mad and all he used to say was, 'Farokh, you'll have me bloody shot. Don't do that again.'

Minnie's fears would seem to have been well grounded and Farokh's choice of a cricketing career almost certainly enhanced his life expectancy.

On arrival at the R.A. Podar College of Commerce and Economics Farokh immediately became captain of the college team on the insistence of Professor Chandgadkar, who was trying to ensure that Podar became a major cricket-playing college:

In the past the only two colleges that really dominated were St Xavier's College and Elphinstone College, both located in the centre of Bombay town. All the Test cricketers came from these two colleges. Professor Chandgadkar, in his wisdom, wanted to make Podar like these colleges. By the time I was a student there were another two leading cricket colleges – the Ramnarain Ruia College, which was right next door to Podar, and Siddharth who were the college champions. There was a hell of a lot of needle with Ruia; Wadekar and a lot of other top players came from there so we had a number of battles against them. In every year that I captained Podar we reached the semi-finals of the inter-college tournament, and sometimes the final, though we never became the champions. The finals were a big thing, with a holiday granted for both the colleges.

Chandgadkar's initiatives certainly led to a blossoming of cricketing talent at Podar, with Ravi Shastri, Dilip Vengsarkar, Sanjay Manjrekar and many more following in Farokh's footsteps.

Learning to fly, playing cricket and academic studies led to action-packed and exhausting days:

I would go early in the morning to the college. Perhaps before studies there would be an air-wing session so I would go flying. College would start at nine, nine-thirty, ten o'clock. It was a full day and lessons would finish at four in the afternoon. At three o'clock we had our cricket practice so I had to miss the last lecture. You were allowed to miss college for cricket practice, and we used to practice until late. We never went to the pub afterwards. There was no such thing as going out for a drink and we were too tired to do anything. Sun set at seven o'clock or so and I used to go home and man was I hungry. Mum used to have a really good meal and then I had to do my homework or whatever and lights were off by nine o'clock. There was no television in those days, no television to watch. Flying, studies, cricket and bed was the order of the day – and time to meet the odd girlfriend for a bit of innocent flirting!

One character who left a clear impression on Farokh's mind was the college cricket peon or servant, named Parab:

He was a lovely chap. He would clean your kit and your boots so they were bright and spotless, one hell of a nice guy, the custodian of the team and he did it all for the love of the game. He rarely got tips because we were all broke in those days. When his son got married I was invited as the guest of honour and he still gets in touch when I visit Bombay. But although he was a servant I always treated him with respect and because I was the captain that meant the rest of the team treated him with respect also. He was loved by everyone and a mad keen supporter of the team, watching every match.

At the other end of the social scale Farokh pays tribute to the assistance of Professor M.V. Chandgadkar, who was the Vice Principal of Podar College and the cricket enthusiast who had made the offer of a free ship if Farokh would join his college:

He was very instrumental in my life, an exceedingly nice man who made a tremendous impact on my career as well as helping me with my studies. He was very enthusiastic, very knowledgeable, a lovely, lovely person. He also had ambitions to join the Bombay Cricket Association on one of the committees. The problem was he was virtually unknown outside academic circles and to get onto the committee you needed votes from the various clubs in and around Bombay – just as if someone wants to get onto the committee at Lancashire they need support from clubs like Accrington or Blackburn. Well I was known to the clubs so I used to enjoy taking the afternoon off from college and go canvassing support for my professor. He got elected and the next thing I knew was that he had become the honorary secretary of the Bombay Cricket Association. From that he rose to the status of All India; he was the secretary of the Cricket Board of Control in India. He deserved every honour but has sadly passed away.

Almost as soon as Farokh began playing for his college team he was selected for the Bombay University side and in December 1958 he played his first first-class match for the Combined Universities against the touring West Indies. This tour has been likened to the eleventh-century invasion by Mahmud of Gazni who swept down onto the Indian plains from his retreat in Afghanistan to plunder, loot, massacre and desecrate. The West Indies team included two young fast bowlers, Wesley Hall and Roy Gilchrist, whose ferocity and sustained aggression struck terror into the hearts of the gentlemanly Indians. Mihir Bose compared the tour to warfare where the Indians were equipped with pea-shooters against the latest machine guns of the West Indians. He describes the months of this tour as 'the darkest in Indian cricket history'.

Wes Hall was a tall, muscular Barbadian the pace of whose deliveries has been compared to a speeding bullet. Christopher Martin Jenkins wrote of his 'long athletic approach, with eyes bulging, teeth glinting, and a crucifix swinging from his chest, an aesthetic joy to the spectator, but an intimidating sight for the batsman'. Shortly after the Indian tour Wes Hall was to achieve a Test hat-trick against Pakistan at Lahore. Wisden has described Gilchrist as 'the most frightening fast bowler in history' and 'an untamed Jamaican rude boy'. He was once accused of branding his wife and when questioned about the incident replied that 'The iron was not hot'. When he arrived in India his days as an international cricketer were numbered, for he was sent home after the Indian section of the tour for refusing to stop bowling beamers and being involved in a knife incident. Both Hall and Gilchrist were capable of bowling six bouncers in an over.

Along with this terrifying pace attack the West Indies team included a plethora of batting talent such as Rohan Kanhai, whose first century and highest Test score of 256 were achieved in six and a half hours at Calcutta in January 1959, and Garfield Sobers. The twenty-two-year-old Sobers had recently scored 365 not out in the third Test against Pakistan at Kingston on 1 March 1958, surpassing Hutton's world record Test innings of 364 for England against Australia at The Oval in 1938. Sobers' record was to stand for thirty-six years until broken by Brian Lara. The West Indies met the Combined Universities in a three-day match between 20 and 22 December 1958.

By the time of this match held at Nagpur, 2 Tests had already been played at Bombay and Kanpur with the first ending up as a draw and the second as a 203-run win for the West Indies. The tour side was just getting into its stride.

The original intention was that the West Indies would field a Second XI since they were only to play students. But on the eve of the match the local mayor, who had little knowledge of the game, claimed in his exuberance that the visitors would be facing a side superior to the Indian Test team. This ensured that the West Indies fielded a full-strength side and changes were made overnight to include the frontline fast bowlers.

The West Indies batted first, scoring 368 runs for 4 wickets declared in 66 overs – almost a run per ball, with Sobers scoring 161. Farokh's scorecard contribution was to catch Rodriguez off the bowling of Das Gupta. It was no wonder that the Combined Universities were then wiped out for 49 in 17.1 overs with every batsman bar one falling victim to Gilchrist or Hall. Farokh

Right: The 'Speeding Bullet' (Wes Hall).

Below: Farokh with Wes Hall and Gary Sobers.

failed to score and was one of three batsmen bowled by Gilchrist for a duck. With the exception of Mitter, who scored 17, the highest score was 5. The West Indian onslaught must have been quite terrifying as these were the days before protective padding and helmets. The only visible protection for the batsmen was white cotton gloves with soft rubber spikes along the finger pieces. After this humiliation the Combined Universities were then forced to follow on:

The first three batsmen were seriously injured – one with a fractured collar bone, another with a blow to the head and the third with a fractured arm. The West Indians were very keen to get us out quickly because they wanted to go to the races. There was an important race on that afternoon, a 2000 Guineas or something like that, and they just wanted to shoot these little kids out as quickly as possible and they tried their damnest. But we were stubborn and I was the joint highest scorer with 29 and altogether we scored 167. To me that 29 was like getting over a hundred or a double century because the bowling was so tight.

If the touring team were frustrated by this resistance then they certainly took out their wrath in the Third Test, subjecting the Indians to their worst defeat in Test history at Calcutta. The West Indies won by an innings and 336 runs.

From this point onwards Farokh continued playing college and university cricket and matches for the CCI. His next major breakthrough came when he was selected to play for the Indian Starlets on their tour of Pakistan in the spring of 1960. The Starlets were like the England 'A' Team, a group of promising young players many of whom would be expected to graduate to Test cricket. Their principal opposition was the Pakistan Eaglets. Farokh played in 5 of the 7 matches, scoring 110 runs, with a highest score of 71. But his main work was behind the stumps:

This was a very significant tour and the manager was Lala Amarnath, an ex-India captain and a great player. He had decided to select me for the tour after seeing me in the nets at the Brabourne Stadium during the Sunday rest-day of the Third Test against Australia. He was the Chairman of the Indian Selection Committee as well which made it even more significant because if players could impress him it was a stepping stone in the right direction towards international stardom. So I had one hell of a tour and almost every match I would take 5 or 6 catches or stumpings, some of them quite brilliant too. I was on my toes because I was determined to do well in that series. At every official function that we used to go to Lala Amarnath would say as he introduced me: 'This is Farokh Engineer, the next Indian wicketkeeper for years to come.' The Chairman of Selectors endorsing me officially time and again – wow, I was riding on a high and every time he said that it made me even more determined to play better. This was a great experience for me and it was wonderful that Lala Amarnath was being impressed. He would introduce me to his friends as a star. 'Here is a star,' he would say, 'he is going to be my wicketkeeper, he is top class, there is no-one who has been like him, there is no-one who will be like him, he is the business.' And I was on a roll. When we got back from the tour, within two months, because of politics in Indian cricket, Lala Amarnath was dropped from the Selection Committee and suddenly a new, fresh face appeared who had never seen me play and I had to start from scratch all over again. But after a couple of years Amarnath came back to the selection panel and I was one of the first ones he picked.

Farokh's progression towards a place in the Test side was initially blocked by two rivals, Naren Tamhane and then Budhi Kunderan. Tamhane was India's first-choice wicketkeeper between 1955 and 1960. His temperament was the very opposite of Farokh's: neat and tidy without a hint of flamboyance, showmanship or brilliance. Farokh respected his methods while realising that he himself belonged to a different school of wicketkeeping:

Tamhane was regarded as an exceedingly safe wicketkeeper. He interpreted his role as being strictly behind the stumps and nowhere else. Within his range he was a highly proficient player. But he wasn't a diver, he regarded first or leg slip as definitely someone else's job. There were no acrobatics with Tamhane. So this was the scenario: I had to do something brilliant, I had to go for second-slip catches to get noticed. I was desperate to be known as a better wicketkeeper than Tamhane because he was the established Indian wicketkeeper for years and to dislodge a person overnight took a lot of guts.

Tamhane was regarded by Wisden as 'quietly efficient' and he achieved a tally of 35 catches and 16 stumpings in 21 Tests, but his batting was unexceptional, with one Test half century and an average of only 10.23. He was finally dropped in favour of Budhi Kunderan who scored a gutsy and brilliant 71 in his second Test against Australia at the Corporation Stadium, Madras, in January 1960. Kunderan also achieved a double century on his Ranji Trophy debut at Delhi in February 1960, only the second player to have done so at that time. His 192 against England in the First Test at Madras in January 1964 still stands as the highest score by an Indian wicketkeeper. Kunderan was a cricketing adventurer with a carefree approach to the game, who was only prevented from enjoying a prolonged Test match career by the selectors' eventual preference for Farokh Engineer:

Kunderan and I were in the same cricketing academy at the Brabourne Stadium; we were the two honorary members appointed by CCI and we were both aspiring Test cricketers. But while Budhi Kunderan was an outstanding batsman and a brilliant cover-point fielder he was not really a Test-class wicketkeeper. So both our futures were going parallel and we were both making good progress towards Test cricket. But he joined a team called Indian Railways who were looking for a wicketkeeper at the time so they made Kunderan virtually into a wicketkeeper. Armarnath was involved with the Railways side and he dropped Tamhane and picked Kunderan for India. When he scored 71 in his second Test match I thought, 'I've had it here'.

Kunderan's preferment was to be short-lived, however, for on the Starlets tour Lala Amarnath came to appreciate the superior wicketkeeping skills of Engineer. As soon as Amarnath returned to the Selection Committee in 1961 it was only a matter of time before Farokh was selected for the national squad. Once he was selected for India he experienced an immediate confirmation of the status of his new position:

Everyday I was travelling by train from Dadar to Churchgate station. This was the station at the end of the line and was situated close to the financial and commercial heart of the city. I would then walk onto the Brabourne Stadium for an afternoon of cricket practice. Everyday I used to travel on this crowded train with my little pads, bat, gloves and all my worldly possessions. Every evening I would return in this crowded train and sometimes used to literally hang outside the carriage because I couldn't get into the compartment for the numbers of people. Hanging out of the train was quite safe because there was a wooden platform and something to hold on to but the train used to go at 60 to 70 miles per hour. I would hang on with my pads, bat and things. The day my photo came in the papers with the announcement that I had been selected to play for India it was amazing. When I arrived at the station there was a crowd of people who formed themselves around me either just gazing or asking questions. Normally when the train approached the station they would make a collective rush for the compartment but just because I was newly selected for the Indian cricket squad they made sure that I went in first and the person next to me would wipe the seat before I sat down. Then they all rushed to try and sit near me to talk. And I thought, it's not a bad game this. You've got a lot of importance. Being a Test match cricketer in India you are treated like a god. But, like Brazil in football, if you did well you would be praised to the skies, but if you had a bad day they would bury you as well. Luckily I had more good days than bad.

In the course of his cricketing career Farokh was to come across numerous confirmations of his new status. The Indian cricket team were regarded in much the same way as film idols and pop stars. One such occasion was on New Year's Eve 1974 when the West Indies were touring India:

It was the Calcutta Test and I had batted that day, scored some runs and was out. I knew that I could afford to relax a little and celebrate during the evening. Together with Alvin Kallicharran and Clive Lloyd I went out to a party. We weren't back that late but we thought we would see the new year in and it must have been just after midnight. As we were being driven back to the Grand Hotel we saw hundreds of people crowding round the front entrance. We were on a 10.30 p.m. curfew and didn't want to be noticed so we told the driver to go round to the back entrance. But there were just as many people here waiting to catch a glimpse of their favourite player or players. We were spotted and they began chanting 'Kallicharran', 'Lloyd', 'Engineer'. I had to plead with them to be quiet – after all I didn't want to be dropped for the next Test. They wanted autographs and I told them that if they were quiet and stood in a straight line (which stretched right up to Chowringee, one of the main streets in Calcutta) then we would sign for them. And, of course, a plain signature wasn't good enough; they wanted 'best wishes', and the three of us gave them what they wanted and we were hours sitting on the steps, signing away.

Cult status was a mixed blessing, however, and could lead to potentially dangerous situations:

It must have been 1961 and we had just played a Test match at Kanpur. We then had to take the train to Delhi since India Airlines were on strike. As we approached Agra station we could see the Taj Mahal in the distance. A number of us had never visited the monument so we decided to make a detour. Kunderan, who was twelfth man, kindly offered to take our bags to the Delhi hotel. The rest of us left the train at Agra. There were thirty or forty persons at the station and we signed autographs before jumping into a taxi. Before we had travelled much more than half a mile along the road a police car drove up beside us to warn of some 2,000 people who had gathered at the entrance awaiting the arrival of the Indian team. News had spread like lightning. I assured the officer that this was nothing to worry about for they were our supporters and only wanted to touch us or acquire an autograph or two. We were allowed to continue. Another couple of miles along the road and this second police car approached us from the opposite direction with all sirens blazing. This time the officer was covered in stripes and stars and literally pleaded with us to backtrack. Some 20,000 persons had now collected outside the monument entrance and another 20,000 were sure to be on their way. The officer could not guarantee our safety or promise to control the crowds. He feared a stampede and possible casualties. We didn't want to be the cause of a disaster so we made our way back to the station and spent some six hours holed up in a pokey waiting room. Such is the price of success.

As part of the national squad Farokh was on the brink of international acclaim and, following a sound performance against the MCC for Combined Universities in late October 1961, he was selected for the First Test against England to be played at the Brabourne Stadium on 11-16 November.

four

International Cricket

At the time Farokh was first selected to play for his country India were regarded as the 'whipping boys of international cricket'. The game was dominated by England, Australia and the West Indies. To date India had played 52 Test matches against these opponents and won only twice, both occasions being on home soil. This was to be the eighth series between India and England. Memories still rankled from the First Test at Leeds in 1952 when at the beginning of their second innings India had lost 4 wickets without scoring, the worst start in Test history, and the 5-0 whitewash of 1959. Freddie Trueman had stung national pride with his jibe that Indians could not bat and more recently English critics had dubbed the Indian team the 'dull dogs of cricket'. Too many of the Indian cricketing fraternity regarded the English team as superior, if not invincible, and this deferential, almost defeatist, attitude led to defensive and negative play. The order of the day was not to lose. It was far better to draw than risk a defeat. At the First Test at Trent Bridge in June 1959 India had taken six and a half hours to score 206 – a depressing display of slow, boring, uninspiring cricket. One view of English team selection was that in view of the poor quality of the opposition, it was unnecessary to field a full-strength team on the subcontinent. Certainly the side of the 1961-62 tour was without Cowdrey, Trueman and Statham. But the England team was a strong batting side despite Cowdrey's absence and since local conditions favoured spin bowlers it was perhaps decided to conserve the energies of England's pace-bowling attack. England fielded full-strength sides against India in England.

There were signs of a more aggressive approach to the game amongst some younger Indian players. Both Budhi Kunderan and Salim Durani were determined to dispence with the old ways by which occupation of the crease, time-buying and dogged defence seemed to be the approved qualities for a Test batsman. Perhaps the defining innings of the new approach was Kunderan's sparkling 71 scored against Australia in the Fourth Test at Madras in January 1960. Kunderan recalled that after scoring 14 runs in the first over

Introducing a Test cricketer.

'the whole crowd started screaming'. As the slashing continued so the Australian abuse escalated in terms that Kunderan could not understand, but the young hero had captured the imagination of the Indians with his spontaneous, colourful and exciting play. Farokh Engineer had very similar ideas about the nature of cricket.

Farokh was selected for India principally on the grounds of his wicketkeeping skills:

I suppose I had a different approach to wicketkeeping from those who had kept wicket for India before. My approach was more on the offensive in the sense that I got involved a lot more in the game than previous wicketkeepers. The existing conventions were very safe and sound. A wicketkeeper was not supposed to drop a catch but neither was he expected to try something out of the ordinary that was apparently out of his reach. A dive was unheard of. There was a first slip, a second slip, a third slip, a fourth slip and a gully. For opening bowlers the wicketkeeper stood well back, took his ball and gave it to the first slip, who gave it to the second slip, and so on. It was a bit boring, like a time-honoured ritual. When I was behind the stumps I recommended getting rid of the first and second slip with the result that two fielders could be used elsewhere. I had a longer reach, I was fitter and I could dive and reach for those balls which other keepers never dreamt of diving for for fear of missing a catch. I know I dropped one or two but I took more catches and made a position for myself. My most serious competitor was Kunderan, who also used to dive for catches and go for the first and second slip balls, but he was a far better fielder than wicketkeeper and I think it's a great pity that the selectors did not stick with him for his batting and brilliant fielding.

Unfortunately, on the eve of the Test match disaster struck:

The Indian manager was of the opinion that since England had fast bowlers we needed to do some practice against fast bowling. We didn't really have anyone apart from the young Desai to bowl bouncers of Test class, so he invited other bowlers to come and bowl from way beyond the popping crease to make the balls appear quicker in order to sharpen the batsman's reflexes. This would prepare us for the bouncers we would certainly be facing the next day. It was like a series of deliberate no-balls, bowling from 16 to 17 yards. By the time my turn came to bat it was getting late, it was twilight and the light was bad. A lovely gentleman by the name of Raj Singh Dungarpur, who was one of the princes, came on to bowl. He was one of the quickest around those days, even from 22 yards. He bowled a bouncer and I tried to hook it. I was a compulsive hooker and just couldn't leave the ball alone but this time my good friend Raj Singh got the better of me as I mistimed the hit and it came off the top edge of my bat and went straight onto my right eye. I cut my eye rather badly. I was so shocked and disappointed. My Dad gave me stitches and applied ice to the cut but told me that I wouldn't be able to play the next morning. But I was absolutely insistent to the contrary for I was so eager to play. So he told me to report for duty the next morning and let the captain decide. But he added that from a medical point of view I couldn't play: 'You can't keep wicket with one eye, you are nervous as it is and playing with two eyes is bad enough.' Anyway, with my eye the size of a balloon I reported myself fit claiming that I was fully recovered and went out to have a knock. As soon as my captain and everyone else became aware of my condition they said that I would be letting my team down as well as myself if I went out to play. So I had to sit out the First Test and let my friend Kunderan take my place.

Unluckily for Kunderan, while he took 3 catches and made 2 stumpings, he failed to impress with the bat, scoring only 5 runs. The match ended in a draw. Farokh's place was secure for the Second Test, to be held at Green Park, Kanpur, during the first week of December. The walk out to the crease was to prove an education, and provided Farokh with a useful lesson in self-control:

England had this bowler called Tony Lock and the evening before the Kanpur Test he had been very friendly with me at the Governor's cocktail party: he had congratulated me on my selection and we had a glass of pop together. He seemed an extremely nice chap. When I went out to bat he was at the bowler's end and I had to pass him to get to my crease. As I was so nervous I looked up to Lock for some reassurance and inspiration because I thought the guy was so friendly. But he absolutely scowled at me, bombarded me with the rudest words you can hope to hear, four-letter words were flying, almost racist, certainly unprintable. Why was he doing this to me, it was such a personal assault? I became puzzled and annoyed. When I reached the crease there were 3 balls left in the over and I was surrounded by all the English players. Polly Umrigar was at the non-striker's end. The first ball, I was sure, was on middle stump, so I put my left foot forward and swiped it, partly on account of the close fielding and partly through sheer nervousness and immaturity. Luckily, it caught the middle of the bat and went for 4 runs – and, if my memory is correct, I dealt with the next 2 balls in similar fashion. Polly Umrigar walked up to me and said, 'Forget the screaming crowds, you need to buckle down here and restrain yourself a bit.' By the end of the day's play I was on 18 not out and had helped to increase the run-rate which up to that point was lamentably slow. The next day I batted for less than an hour but delivered the odd ball to the boundary. Lock maintained his verbal barrage and, in the end, talked me out of my wicket: when I was on 33, I tried to hit him over the top and jumped out of my crease to go for it, but missed the ball. I was stumped. But we were about to declare so there wasn't much loss and I didn't let my team down. That

With Prime Minister Nehru.

evening there was another function. India is full of cocktail parties and at Test matches there are always various get-togethers in the marquees and all sorts of things, too much of that in fact. Lock came up to me and said, 'Well played you bugger, but I almost got you out first ball.' I said, 'Tony, you were so nice to me the other evening, why were you sledging me, you knew I was nervous as hell when walking into bat?' He said, 'I sure knew that and I was making you even more nervous because I wanted your wicket and you almost gave it to me. You were swiping from mid-stump and had you missed it you would have been out first ball.' That incident was a great education to me for when Lock said that he had almost unnerved me I thought that I must never lose my cool out there again.

India had scored 467 for 8 declared, their highest ever Test total at Kanpur, and then England were bowled out for 244 with Farokh catching Richardson off the bowling of Gupte and Allen from the bowling of Borde. England were then forced to follow on but scored 497 for 5 wickets and the match ended in a draw. Farokh had made a creditable start and was virtually assured of a place in the side for the rest of the series. The Third Test played at Delhi also ended in a draw but the Fourth and Fifth Tests resulted in victories for India. It was during the Fifth Test played at the Corporation Stadium, Madras, that Farokh made his first major impression with the bat at Test level, scoring his first half century and hitting the new England fast bowler Barry Knight for 16 in one over. This performance, combined with his work behind the stumps, ensured selection for the tour of the West Indies that followed almost immediately upon the departure of the English touring side. The series against England had ended in a 2-0 victory for India, the first time India had won a series against a major cricketing nation and only the third series that India had won in her cricketing history. England had been forced to realise that India were becoming more competitive than in the past and that to field a less than full-strength side in India was to run an increased risk of defeat. India may not have arrived on the world-class scene but they could no longer be dismissed with Trueman-style contempt.

Farokh soon became an integral part of the Indian team:

I was received exceedingly well by all the players and earned their respect almost immediately. New Test players could take a considerable time to be accepted and I felt privileged to be made to feel so at home so quickly – and by some of the senior members of the squad who not so long ago had been my boyhood heroes.

In part this easy transition into the national team was a result of Farokh being the wicketkeeper:

The most important position in the field is the wicketkeeper. If the wicketkeeper's chips are down the whole team's heads are down. He is the centrifugal point; he either makes or breaks the team. His performance picks up the team by example, by conversation, by morale-boosting methods. He's the one person all the players look to, they have their eyes on him all the time because everyone throws the ball to the wicketkeeper. He is most in the action; he is the focal point, right in the middle. He is surrounded by everybody, he watches everybody and certainly everybody watches him. The team looks up to the wicketkeeper to a certain extent because apart from the captain it is the wicketkeeper who controls and advises the slip fielders and suggests a rearrangement of the field placings, or even bowling changes, as the wicketkeeper knows exactly what the bowler is doing and how the pitch is reacting, enabling him to judge quickly a batsman's strengths and weaknesses.

It obviously helped Farokh in this role that he was such an extrovert:

I haven't come across an introvert wicketkeeper – maybe in the past there were some, yes, my predecessors, for that matter – and since my playing days nearly all the keepers have been extroverts such as Alan Knott and Rodney Marsh. Only Bob Taylor was a bit of an introvert I would say. Kirmani was certainly an extrovert, as was Wasim Bari of Pakistan. Nowadays all the wicketkeepers seem to be colourful characters and pretty good batsmen too. Being an extrovert certainly helps – most times.

Looking back on his first Test match colleagues, Farokh has particular memories of his boyhood hero, Polly Umrigar, together with the all-rounder Salim Durani. Polly Umrigar is described as 'a great inspiration, a great friend and a great guidance factor'. He was still one of Farokh's heroes and had scored 147 not out during the Kanpur Test against England, becoming the first Indian to pass 3,000 runs in Test cricket. Farokh remembers that Polly was his room-mate during the England series:

In accordance with the curfew, we would go to bed quite early and about 10.30 or 11 o'clock there was a knocking. It was a huge room and Polly's bed was in the opposite corner to my own. Being the junior pro it was my prerogative to get up and answer the door, you don't expect the senior player to do that. There is a lot of respect for senior players in India (I don't think that respect exists in England or anywhere else – you can't imagine Dennis Lillee deferring to his elders) so Polly knew that I would get up to open the door. But when I opened the door there was no one there and this happened twice until I heard Polly chuckling and realised that he had been knocking the bed frame. He even arranged to have a cable sent to me purporting to come from a girl in Bombay that I was fairly keen on. It read 'can't wait for you to get back to Bombay, will come and collect you from the airport'. Well, of course, she wasn't there and all the other lads who had been let in on the joke said to me, 'Something must have happened, why don't you give her a ring?' She didn't know what I was going on about and they were all splitting themselves with laughter.

Salim Durani was one of the principal architects of India's victory over England in the 1961-62 series, taking 8 and 10 wickets successively in the country's triumphs at Calcutta and Madras:

Durani was an excellent all-rounder, a flamboyant character, a great bowler – in fact, I thought he was one of the best. People in England unfortunately never had the chance to see him except in the minor leagues. He could turn the ball on any wicket and was a very attractive batsman – the kind of guy who would hit 2 sixes and then if the crowd were shouting for a third he would go for it even if he was risking his wicket. Salim was a very entertaining player and a very good-looking chap; he even appeared in a film later on.

Contact with the English tourists was limited:

With the President of India, Dr Radhakrishnan, flanked by Durani and Pataudi.

There wasn't much socialising. The English team would stay in the best five-star hotels and they used to go down to the bar drinking. We couldn't afford it and we weren't allowed alcoholic drinks in those days, especially during Test matches. There wasn't much mixing except at the match when we used to sit together in the players' enclosure and exchange ideas and thoughts. Perhaps we would take them sight-seeing or if they wanted to do some shopping we would help them with our contacts.

Apart from Tony Lock, three other members of the English side made an impression: the wicketkeeper J.T. Murray, the right-handed batsman Ken Barrington and the captain, Ted Dexter:

John Murray was an excellent person and a pretty safe wicketkeeper. I never saw him do anything brilliant. He was similar in style to Tamhane. John Murray's characteristic mannerism was to straighten his cap before every single ball. I could watch him from miles away and immediately recognise his style.

I remember Ken Barrington because of the Australian cricketer Ken Mackay who had recently toured India with the Australian Test team. Mackay would always chew the cud on the field. His jaws were very strong and he just kept on chewing and chewing like a cow. This guy also used to walk like a gorilla with swinging arms and his eccentric movements had amused the Indian crowds. When Barrington was fielding he used to imitate Mackay during the Test match and the crowds just loved it and they really took to him.

Dexter was a flamboyant character. I will never forget during one of the Test matches I was at the non-striker's end and whoever was batting played a defensive stroke. I was just lazing away and the ball went to Dexter. He fielded it and threw the ball to the bowler's end so quickly I was completely off guard. I was out of my crease and hadn't grounded my bat and the ball missed the stumps by a whisker. That was a great lesson to me to keep my eyes open all of the time. But Ted Dexter was a great man with a very classy style. He looked like a great player and he made some shots that were completely out of the textbook with such class and perfection, but he got out to some rash shots as well. They called him Lord Edward, very upper class, spoke very well, an ideal English captain and a successful and popular president of the MCC.

There was little time for reflection after the England series for almost immediately the Indian team left for the Caribbean. The First Test at Port of Spain, Trinidad, against the West Indies took place just one month after the final Madras Test against England. India had had little time to prepare and the high expectations created by the successes against England were soon dashed. But this was no ordinary West Indies team. In fact it has been described as 'perhaps the best all-round side the West Indies have ever had'. In the First Test the West Indies won by 10 wickets, bowling out the Indians for 98 in their second innings. Farokh lost his wicket cheaply in both innings to Lance Gibbs. Although the West Indies also won the Second Test at Sabina Park, Kingston, Jamaica, by an even greater margin – an innings and 18 runs – Farokh had a much better time with the bat, scoring 53 and 40. Many of these runs were made at the expense of Wes Hall:

No Indian player had ever hooked Wes Hall and I was hooking him fairly regularly during the Jamaica Test, so much so that his dear old mum, when we reached Barbados, asked him, 'Who is this brave, young Indian batsman called Engineer? Can you bring him home to meet me?' And one day after the game in Barbados, Wes said to me, 'Farokh, if you are not doing anything my mum would be very happy if you were to come with me to see her.' And I thought, 'Me, going to Wes Hall's house, that will be a great experience.' In the little car his head was almost reaching through the roof and I went to his little place and saw his frail little mum there: 'You're the man whose been hitting my son all over the place. Not many people have done that,' she said. 'Yeh, mum,' interrupted Wes, 'he's trashing me too much.' Ever since that occasion Wes has been a very dear friend.

Farokh also began a friendship with the West Indian captain, Frank, later Sir Frank, Worrell. Worrell was one of the greatest West Indian cricketers, the first

Sabina Park, March 1962.

black captain who, according to Wisden 'did much to bind together the Caribbean nations and dispel the island factions within the side'. In 51 Tests he averaged close to 50 with the bat but it was the elegant manner of his play that impressed spectators. Neville Cardus wrote that he never made a crude or ungrammatical stroke, while to Sir Learie Constantine 'Worrell was poetry'. After his early death at the age of forty-two there was a memorial service in Westminster Abbey. Farokh recalls:

My first meeting with the great Frank Worrell was at Kingston airport. The great man who I had heard so much about turned up to receive the Indian cricket team. Later that same day I was by the pool at the Flamingo Hotel in Kingston. The Test match was two or three days away. The rest of the team had been to the West Indies before so they all had friends, girlfriends or whatever and had gone off to parties. I was alone by the pool. And the great man walks towards me and says, 'Hello Farokh'. I was surprised that he even knew my name. 'Hello Mr Worrell,' I replied, 'Ah, call me Frank,' he said, and asked where everyone was. I told him that they had gone out. 'Have you had enough of your swim?' he asked, 'Come on and get changed. You're coming out with me.' I was so overwhelmed. Me going out with the great

Frank Worrell.

Frank Worrell! I tried to excuse myself saying that I was expecting somebody and this and that, but he knew I was bluffing and told me to go and get changed. I couldn't wait to get my shorts on. We went out in his white Jaguar and he got so drunk that night that in the end I had to drop him off home. I remember Velda, his wife, and I had to literally carry him out of the car and tuck him in his bed. I thought to myself, 'Christ, the great Frank Worrell, I have put him to bed.' After that Frank and Velda remained exceedingly good friends until Frank passed away. Whenever I went to Barbados for cricket or business, I would always call on Velda and we would go up to Frank's grave and put some flowers there. I would always take a carton of cigarettes for her and she would invite me round for dinner with cricketing friends of Frank. He was a great, great man and she a great, great lady. Sadly they have both now passed away.

Between the Second and Third Test matches the Indian tourists played a colony game against Barbados. This match ended the Test career and nearly the life of the Indian captain, Nari Contractor. Contractor had been appointed captain for the series against Pakistan in 1960-61, becoming, at 26, the youngest Indian captain. He had started his first-class career by scoring a century in each innings for Gujarat against Baroda in the Ranji Trophy in November 1952. His greatest success as a captain came with the historic victory over England in the eighth series but all was to change following a short delivery from Charlie Griffith.

This incident will always remain so clear in my mind and it appears as if it happened only yesterday. I'm sure that the players still have nightmares about it, especially as Nari came so close to death. I remember so vividly when Charlie Griffith bowled this bouncer. Contractor wasn't a hooker of the ball, he was a leaver and he used to duck bouncers very effectively if I may say so – he was one of the topmost opening batsmen in the world. And on that occasion, on that wicket at The Oval in Barbados, the ball did not rise as high as Contractor expected it to. With Griffith's speed the ball normally rose very high, way above Contractor's head, but on that particular occasion the ball seemed to skid right into Nari. Whenever a bowler's action is a little debatable the ball usually skids at you. This particular ball skidded in at around 100mph. There were no measuring machines, but it was certainly very, very quick and Nari ducked thinking the ball would go over his head, but unfortunately the ball just skidded and hit him straight on the side of his head, right in the temple, and the ball just dropped dead right by his feet. That showed that it wasn't a glancing blow because a glancing blow wouldn't have been too bad but it was the full thud of a 100mph delivery and made a full impact just by the side of his brain. He buckled down, his knees gave way and he was almost on the ground. Everyone rushed up to him including all the players in the dressing room. They knew that something very serious was wrong. Yes, we could even hear the thud of the ball hitting his skull with only a little cap for protection. This was real danger, everyone saw red and we all ran out to the crease. To everybody's surprise Nari got up again and said 'I'm all right, I'm all right, leave me alone, leave me alone'. As we were reluctantly beginning to come off the pitch we couldn't help noticing blood trickling out of his nose and ears and that's a sure sign that the skull is fractured. That was when Nari collapsed and we had to carry him into the dressing room. There was no top surgeon in Barbados available at the time so the manager had to make phone calls to New York to fly a surgeon over to operate. To my recollection a surgeon did fly over from New York. Now Nari was of a certain blood group that wasn't very common so the whole team went to the hospital prepared to give blood. I must say, hats off to the great Frank Worrell: he was at the hospital all night having given blood himself to see if it matched with Nari's group. Nari was such a popular person and the way he had the team round him was superb. He was very brainy indeed and an excellent opening batsman. His dropping like a ninepin was a sorry sight, a deplorable sight from a fellow teammate. And it made us aware of the dangers of the game. You just couldn't afford to take a ball anywhere on your body at that speed. You're going to break your bones – your elbow, a wrist, your forearm, your shoulder and worst of all, your head. It was a real eye-opener.

After several emergency operations, Contractor survived, but a tantalum plate was inserted in his skull. Farokh recalls that whenever he enquired about his injury Contractor replied, 'What do you mean? My skull is a lot stronger than yours.' While Contractor was never selected for another Test match, he continued to play first-class cricket with considerable distinction until the 1970-71 season. It might have been thought that an injury of this kind would have hastened the introduction of protective gear, but the position of a batsman facing fast bowling remained a perilous one:

Protective gear wasn't even thought of in those days. We had rubber pimpled gloves, a pink plastic box and if you were lucky enough to have a little towel as a thigh pad that was the only protection. We never had any chest pads or forearm guards, never mind helmets. The plastic box was a flimsy affair and though a lot better than nothing failed to prevent a fast bowler from inflicting severe pain. I well remember being doubled-up by Dennis Lillee when I was playing for the World XI in Perth, perhaps the fastest wicket in the world. The ball nipped back from outside off stump, hit me in the knackers and dropped dead. There were tears in my eyes. It was like being strangled and, of course, everyone was laughing and cracking jokes.

I still say that the introduction of helmets probably saved a lot of lives, certainly, but it decreased the skill of the batsman over the years because to hook a bouncer was a delight to see. The way a batsman handled a bouncer was like a gladiator going out in the arena against a lion and using his skill to protect himself and to kill the lion. With helmets it was like having a padded gladiator, so even if the lion chewed him he would probably survive and people would come to the rescue. More people get hit on the head these days since the introduction of helmets. I've tried a helmet just once in the nets and I wondered how the batsman could even see the ball. It hampers your vision and gives you an uneasy feeling. I certainly wouldn't have been happy with it.

Charlie Griffiths' unfortunate incident with Contractor struck terror into the hearts of some of the Indian batsmen and the day after the injury Farokh was batting with a colleague whose name, for obvious reasons, he wants to keep secret:

We were standing out in the square having faced a couple of overs or so when I noticed my partner was shuffling around in a rather awkward manner. I walked up to him to ask him what the matter was. 'I've messed my pants,' came the reply. 'You're going to have to sort yourself out,' I told him, and suggested we tell the West Indies captain that he needed to go into the pavilion for a few minutes as he was having problems with his box. It turned out to be more than a few minutes. Needless to say it was fear, not a tummy bug, that had produced this unfortunate result.

One member of the Indian touring party provided Farokh with an amusing story – the right-arm fast-medium-pace bowler Vasant Ranjane. Ranjane had made an unforgettable first-class debut when he took 9 for 35, including a hat-trick, and 4 for 36 for Maharashtra against Saurashtra in 1956-57. In the First Test against England played at Bombay in December 1961 Ranjane was the most successful bowler with 4 for 76 in the first innings. He played in just one Test on the West Indies tour at Kingston, where he took the wickets of Hunte, Kanhai, Sobers and Worrell in the first innings for 72 runs. Farokh's anecdote comes from one of the other matches played during this tour:

Ranjane was a good quick bowler but he didn't even know which side of the bat to hold. He wasn't the best of batsmen. On one occasion during the Caribbean tour Ranjane was facing Roy Gilchrist, one of the fastest and maddest of the West Indian bowlers who knew that Ranjane couldn't bat but still kept peppering him with bouncers. It would have been quite enough to have bowled a straight ball, for Ranjane was always backing towards the square leg umpire, but as he was backing the bowler followed him with his delivery and bowled a bouncer just to show off how quick he was against a tailender. The ball went off Ranjane's gloves, off his shoulders and into the hands of the wicketkeeper. As the appeal went up the umpire shouted 'no ball' and, of course, all the fielders stayed on the field. But to everyone's surprise Ranjane started walking back to the pavilion and everyone shouted, including the non-striker, 'Vasant, that was a no ball'. But Ranjane, having obviously had enough of the West Indies bombardment said, 'No, I'm quite happy. There was nothing wrong with the ball.' And off he walked.

five

Indian Domestic Cricket

After the Barbados Test which followed the near-fatal injury to Contractor, Farokh lost his place in the side to Kunderan, who played in the Fourth and Fifth Tests. This made no difference to the course of the series and, despite centuries by both Umrigar and Durani in the Fourth Test, the West Indies won both games, taking the series 5-0. This began a period of nearly three years of Test exile for Farokh. He missed both the home series against England of 1963-64 and the home series against Australia of 1964-65. Losing out to Kunderan was disappointing, but Farokh had the greatest respect for his friend's batting and fielding skills. In the 1963-64 series against England, Kunderan scored 2 centuries, including a 192 in the First Test, together with one half century, and it looked as if his batting alone would secure him selection for the 1964-65 Australian series. But for reasons that defy rational analysis Kunderan and Engineer were displaced by Indrajitsinhji. K.S. Indrajitsinhji was at best a competent wicketkeeper and in the three-match Test series against Australia he scored a grand total of 32 runs in 5 innings. During his months in the wilderness Farokh had to concentrate on domestic cricket.

Selection for the Indian national team has been likened to a form of Russian roulette. Certainly Farokh claims that Indian selection is more influenced by politics and underhand manoeuvrings than in most cricketing countries. The case of the leg-spinner S.P. Gupte amply illustrates the strange principles of Indian selection. According to *The Times* obituary, 'It was said that he laughed too much and failed to show enough respect to his superiors. He was once dropped for turning up in shorts for nets in Madras.' Even more outrageous was the way Gupte was treated following the Third Test against England at Delhi in December 1961. Gupte had already distinguished himself in the series by achieving figures of 5 for 90 during the Second Test, Farokh's Test debut, so ensuring England's first follow-on against India. But all this was to count for nothing, simply because Gupte had the misfortune to be sharing a room with Kripal Singh at the Imperial Hotel in Connaught Circus. Kripal

Singh had telephoned the hotel receptionist and tried to make a date with her. Farokh suspects that there was a connection between this girl and a member of the Cricket Board of Control. She complained to the team manager. Both Singh and Gupte were suspended and Gupte was left out of the touring side to the West Indies and never played Test cricket again. His only crime was to have shared a room with a man who asked a girl out for a drink. He was an unwitting accessory to a piece of innocent flirting, a so-called impropriety. Farokh's general observations on Indian selection are quite uncompromising:

At times it was almost a disgrace, as players who were almost unheard of on some occasions were being drawn into the Test team. How many one-Test wonders are there in India? More than in any other country. Players are keen to be selected for one Test just so they can call themselves a Test cricketer for the rest of their lives. That's their sole ambition, to play once and be branded a Test cricketer, because you are a Test cricketer even if you have played only one game for your country. There was a lot of politically-motivated selection, of favours being returned, it was diabolical. For example, a certain selector would come from a certain zone. The zone might well take the view that if two of its players were not in the Test side then the selector was not doing his job for the zone and he would be replaced. So there would be a lot of wheeling and dealing and it would be quite likely that these two cricketers were not top class, but they would be in the team for reasons best known to themselves or the selectors. The latter wanted to protect their own little cliques and there were so many indirect favours in various forms for them, their families and friends. I would like to think that less of this sort of thing happens nowadays and that the selectors are knowledgeable ex-Test players, but both before and during my time some of the selections were very questionable.

Farokh's personal experience of the vagaries of selection revolve around two episodes, the first of which concerned the selection of Indrajitsinhji as wicketkeeper for the series against Australia in India during 1964-65. Both Kunderan and Engineer were widely acknowledged as better wicketkeepers and batsmen, but somehow Indrajitsinhji was chosen. He certainly had a confident manner reflecting his princely birth and connections with the Ranji family, but perhaps may not have possessed the class of a Test cricketer. Farokh claims that he was 'flabbergasted at the choice, as was the Indian team and much of the cricketing public'. To rub salt into the wound, Farokh remembers playing pool during one afternoon of the Calcutta Test in October 1964:

I was the reserve keeper to Indrajitsinhji for the match at the Eden Gardens Stadium. Since I wasn't playing, I divided my time between watching the cricket, net practices and the odd game of pool in an area near the dressing

At the Brabourne Stadium.

room. I was playing with Barry Jarman, the Australian wicketkeeper. The Chairman of the Selectors strolled into the room and said to me, 'Farokh, instead of playing pool just watch Indrajitsinhji keep wickets and you might learn something from him.' Jarman gave him such a dirty look, for he knew an injustice had been done, that I was worried that he might hit him with the cue and immediately went over to distract him.

After the Australian series Indrajitsinhji was dropped from the national side, making just one more appearance for India when Farokh was injured for the Third Test against New Zealand at Hyderabad in October 1969. Although Indrajitsinhji failed to impress at Test level, he was a major success in the Ranji Trophy while playing for both Delhi and Saurashtra; he was one of the first wicketkeepers to complete 100 dismissals in the national competition and in 1960-61 claimed 23 victims, then the record. Farokh suffered again at the hands of the selectors during the series against the West Indies in India during 1974-75:

The Nawab of Pataudi, the regular captain, was injured during the First Test at Bangalore after dislocating his finger. Indeed, I was injured also but recovered in time for the Second Test to be held in Delhi in December 1974. Pataudi did not and so Gavaskar was made captain. But he too was injured while playing for Bombay and the team arrived in Delhi without a leader. One of the most senior members of the Indian Board of Control, Ram Prakash Mehra, publically announced me as the captain for the match at an official function the evening before and wished me all the best. The papers and radio also announced that I was going to lead the side. The next morning Clive Lloyd, the West Indies captain, came into our dressing room at about nine or nine-thirty in his blazer and said, 'Rookie, let's go and toss'. Somehow I had a sneaking suspicion that something underhand was going on for one of the selectors came up to me and said, 'No Farokh, there is something going on behind your back that I know about but can't speak about so don't go out and toss yet.' Time was getting on, it was now quarter to ten and the umpires were getting impatient, not wanting to delay the start. Suddenly, Chandrasekhar was told that he was being dropped from the team and Venkataraghavan was flown in from Madras minutes before the game to come and captain the team instead of me. Venkataraghavan was very understanding about the situation and said, 'Farokh, I'm sorry, I've just been told'. I certainly wasn't in the mood to go out and open the innings against some of the fastest bowlers in the world after this disappointment. I felt let down, as if my country did not have confidence in me. My suspicions were confirmed that there must be someone who didn't like me very much. I was so crestfallen – one of the major disappointments of my life. I shall never forget how Clive Lloyd came up to me and said, 'Pal, I can imagine the mood you'll be in; I'll be placing the fielders around the boundary.' He knew how disappointed I was and really felt for me. I had no quarrel with Venkataraghavan. He was a very fine off-spinner and is now a top-class umpire – in fact, in my opinion he is the very best. But after that Test he was dropped from the side and Pataudi returned as captain. I did wonder whether whoever arranged this humiliation hoped that I would throw in the towel. Certainly the press and the Indian sporting public were very critical of the strange decision.

Farokh sensed that the fact that he was playing county cricket in England from 1968 did not exactly endear him to the Indian cricketing authorities, though this fact didn't stop the West Indies from appointing a captain from almost identical circumstances. Certainly Farokh did not belong to the deferential school of Indian cricketers. On one occasion he had the audacity to question the travelling arrangements of the Indian national side:

We were playing against the Australians. One Test was in Bombay and the next in Calcutta. The custom was that the Indian team should travel by train, but by train the journey took two and a half days because it was one hell of a long way from the west to east coast. By jet the journey took just four and a half hours. The train fare was actually fifteen rupees more expensive than the plane, and this bought an air-conditioned compartment. I just couldn't understand the reasoning behind the Indian Cricket Board of Control's insistence that we travel by train. The journey was exhausting, because we would be woken up in all the stations during the middle of the night because villagers got to know that the Indian team was passing through and they would bang on the windows to obtain an autograph or two or perhaps the odd photograph. It was lovely seeing them coming from miles all over the place, and great for a player's ego, but not conducive to a restful ride. I spoke out against this custom and pointed out that we were losing two days' practice in Calcutta. The Australians and all foreign teams would always travel by air. But I was regarded as too outspoken. How dare I speak out against the establishment? How dare I even suggest flying when we were supposed to go by train? They regarded me as the naughty boy of the team, the one who refused to toe the line, a troublemaker. I had to be taught a lesson and put in my place. Perhaps that is why I was not allowed to captain the Test Match in Delhi – but I'm more inclined to think that there was a lot more to it than that, I suspect that vindictiveness and favouritism played more than a minor role in this matter.

With selection such a political matter in India, selectors were always looking for any misdemeanour or minor infringement of the rules to justify a partisan decision. They did what they wanted to do and then found their reasons. Zonal obligations often took precedence over what should have been the overriding objective – to select the best side possible to maximise the chances of success on the field. Backscratching, the settling of personal scores and fear of losing influence seem to have been clandestine motives behind the selection or deselection of Test cricketers. Because of disfavour with the cricketing authorities, Farokh was obliged to concentrate on state and zonal cricket between April 1962 and the end of February 1965. In fact, India played no Test cricket between the end of the series in the West Indies which ended in April 1962 and the First Test against England which began in January 1964.

The most important part of first-class domestic cricket in India was and is the Ranji Trophy. This domestic competition, which began in the 1934-35 season, is held in memory of India's most famous cricketer, HH Shri Sir Ranjitsinhji Vibhaji, Jam Sahib of Nawanagar. Ironically, India's principal domestic competition is named after a man who decided to forge his cricketing career in England rather than India, playing for Cambridge University, Sussex and England – but in Ranji's time there was no Indian XI at Test level. Ranji played 15 Tests for England against Australia between 1896 and 1902 with a batting average of 44.95. He scored 154 not out on his Test debut at Old Trafford in 1896 after England had been forced to follow on and was the first player to reach 3,000 runs in an English season in 1899, a feat he repeated the following year. In 1904 Ranji returned to India with a reputation as one of the world's greatest cricketers and three years later became the ruler of Nawanagar.

Despite his sporting talents he never played more than social cricket in India. For the purposes of the Ranji Trophy, India is divided into zones. Farokh played for Bombay, which is in the West Zone. The first stage of the competition consists of a league within each zone. Bombay would play matches against Saurashtra, Baroda, Gujarat and Maharashtra. The top team in the West Zone league would then compete in a knock-out competition against the top teams from the North, South, East and Central Zones. During the 1960s and 1970s up to the 1977-78 season, with the single exception of the 1973-74 season when Karnataka won the Trophy, the winner was Bombay. Indian cricket was to a very large extent Bombay cricket. The Bombay team was full of Test players.

This was the main reason that Farokh did not play much state cricket before being selected for India: Tamhane, the Indian wicketkeeper, was also the regular Bombay wicketkeeper, so once Tamhane was displaced from the state side he was bound to be displaced from the national team. Farokh played his first match in the Ranji Trophy for Bombay against Saurashtra in February 1960, scoring 50. Bombay won by an innings and 207 runs. It was during this game that Farokh was summoned back to Bombay to witness the last hours of his dying mother. In happier times Saurashtra was a popular destination, since the princes used to provide lavish hospitality and rides in their sports cars. Another interesting venue was Baroda:

We used to leave Bombay by train at midnight and arrive there around six o'clock in the morning. Baroda was a prosperous, well-to-do state and we used to stay at the Palace Guest House. The cricket ground was inside the palace grounds where the Maharaja had his own zoo. Monkeys would come into our rooms and take our shaving stuff away, so we always had to close the windows and doors. I remember that the zoo attendant was one-handed and I used to wonder how he had suffered this injury, whether in the war or whatever. In the end I was so curious that I asked him quite blatantly and he replied that his arm had been severed by an alligator. Yet he used to call all the alligators by name and they would swim up to the edge of the water and eat food out of his hand.

Farokh's first first-class century was scored in a Ranji trophy semi-final against Bengal at Calcutta in March 1963. Bengal batted first and were all out for 322. Farokh opened the Bombay innings with Adhikari, scoring 162 in a total of 552 runs, and Bengal were forced to follow on. Bombay won by an innings and 31 runs. The 1962-63 season was a successful one for Farokh, and he averaged 44.76 with the bat. That did not prevent him from receiving a severe reprimand from his captain Polly Umrigar when he was out for 61 when facing the bowling of Sitaram at Delhi:

Sitaram was a tall, lanky bowler who could swing the ball like a banana. He didn't bowl at great pace. In order to counter the swing I used to get out of the crease to hit him over the top or over midwicket or long on. I had made a respectable score and threw my wicket away trying to hit him for another six when Bombay were clearly in the driving seat and in little danger of losing. We still had several wickets left. When I returned to the pavilion Polly Umrigar gave me one of the biggest roastings I have ever received. He was clearly very angry. 'You have let your side down,' he said. 'If Bombay lose today, God help us, you will never play for Bombay again.' That was a great lesson to me, but a lesson that I often failed to heed!

The match in question was between North Zone and West Zone and formed part of the Duleep Trophy. This competition was introduced by the Board of Control for Cricket in India in 1961-62 with the aim of providing a higher level of competition in the domestic programme. The Ranji Trophy had become a completely predictable affair with Bombay winning for fifteen consecutive years. Farokh refers to Bombay as 'the Manchester United of Indian cricket'. The Duleep Trophy would also offer the selectors an additional opportunity to assess form. The competition was a knockout tournament between the five zone sides. During the first ten years of the competition, West Zone won the Trophy five times outright and once jointly with South Zone. The competition was named after Kumar Shri Duleepsinhji, mostly known as Duleep or Mr Smith. He was the nephew of Ranji and, like his uncle, played for Cambridge University, Sussex and England. Also like his uncle he scored a century on his Test debut – a glorious 173 against the Australians in the Lord's Test of 1930. The story is told that Ranji was watching this innings and when Duleep was at last caught from a rash stoke remarked, 'He always was a careless lad'. In the same year Duleep hit 333 in five and a half hours against Northamptonshire at Hove, the highest individual innings played for Sussex. Farokh's most memorable innings in the Duleep Trophy was when he scored 114 before lunch for West Zone against Central Zone at the Brabourne Stadium in February 1965.

It was during a Duleep Trophy match that Farokh had his second encounter with the West Indies fast bowler Roy Gilchrist. Following the 5-0 defeat by the West Indies in 1961-62, the Indian Board imported four West Indian bowlers (Gilchrist, King, Stayers and Watson) in the hope that they would give the Indians practice against fast bowling by participating in the Ranji and Duleep Trophies and by holding coaching clinics in the various zones. There is an unverifiable story that when Gilchrist stepped off the aircraft he was asked by a journalist why, in his opinion, there were no effective Indian fast bowlers. According to legend, Gilchrist replied to the startled questioner, 'Man, you don't eat beef, you don't drink grog, you don't bother with women … how can you have fast bowlers, man?' Gilchrist played for Hyderabad and South Zone. In a match between South Zone and West Zone, Gilchrist was bowling to Engineer:

Gilchrist was bouncing away merrily there – he's fully entitled to bounce – and I hit him for 2 consecutive sixes. The crowds were going wild with excitement, enjoying every moment of the game. On the third ball he just kept running straight towards me, past the umpire and right up to where I was batting. He was bristling with rage and said something like, 'You ugly swine, if you hit me one more time I'll run up to you and ram this red ball into that pretty face of yours', and he even grazed my nose with the seam of the ball. All the players and the two umpires rushed around him to separate us. I said, 'Gilly, when you come out to bat you had better keep a steady eye on those stumps or I will be shoving them where they will really hurt.' These guys only understood one language and that was the language of aggression. You had to handle aggression with aggression. But I was diplomatic; I didn't raise my fists and even spoke to him quite politely. I told him to get on with his bowling. 'You've got a ball in your hand, I've got a bat in mine, you bowl as many bouncers as you like and I'll hit them anywhere I like.'

That night there was a cocktail party and both teams were staying in the same hotel and we all travelled in the same coach. All evening Gilchrist kept glaring and snarling at me. I regarded him as ignorant and completely without class. Shortly after I had retired to my room there was a knock at my door. Funnily enough I had a suspicion it might be him. 'Who's that?' I said. 'It's me, man,' came the reply, and I heard the clinking of glasses. 'What do you want?' I asked. 'I want a drink with you, man,' replied Gilchrist. So I opened the door. He came in and put the two glasses on the table together with a bottle of rum, seemingly oblivious to what had happened between us. He repeated his request. 'Can I have a drink with you, man?' And I thought at the time that this was a lovely gesture from a really ignorant sod. He had behaved so badly all day and yet he suddenly wanted to have a drink. That was his way of saying sorry, though he never actually uttered the word – he was too proud for that. After the glass of rum he started showing me photographs from his wallet of his wife and kids. He was almost in tears and told me how much he was missing them back home. I felt sorry for the guy. He showed that he had some human element after all and after that day I regarded him just a little differently.

There was a second encounter with Gilchrist when both men were playing for an invitation side against the ACC (Associated Cement Company) XI in the final of the Moin-ud-Dowla Gold Cup Tournament played at Hyderabad in October 1962. This tournament, like the Duleep Trophy, served as a useful guide for the Indian selectors and the ACC opposition included players of the stature of Umrigar, Sardesai and Wadekar, while the West Indies fast bowler Lester King joined Prasanna and Manjrekar for the invitation team:

The pitch was really very slow and the ball was hardly carrying to me behind the wickets. Indeed, it was so slow that it was more difficult standing back from the wicket than standing right up at the stumps, even for facing someone of the pace of Gilchrist. So I changed my position and stood right up to the stumps, even with the new ball, and got a stumping off his bowling, a leg-side stumping. And he bowled pretty quickly did Gilly. All my team-mates came running up to congratulate me that I had got a stumping off the fastest bowler in the world, but Gilly was furious. I had blackened his record; no one had taken a wicket off his bowling by standing so close to the stumps before. I had to explain to him that it wasn't his bowling, it was the slowness of the wicket – but he still wasn't happy.

Farokh's principal contribution to Indian domestic cricket was as a wicketkeeper and a batsman. But there were occasions when he bowled the odd over:

We always bowled in the nets, and at first I fancied myself as a quick bowler. I used to take a pretty decent run-up and work up a useful pace and swing the ball too. But I also took to leg spin, leg-spin googlies. I could turn the ball because I have such huge hands and I could give the ball a good rip. I fancied myself as a bowler. Unfortunately, most batsmen fancied me as well! Some of my earliest memories of bowling were in the inter-collegiate games at university, but I also bowled in the Ranji Trophy. This tended to happen when the game was petering out to a draw or was a one-sided affair, the fag-end of a game, never in a serious situation. When I bowled it was just a way to let off steam, to relax a little, to introduce a light-humoured element into the game.

My prize bowling wicket was that of Colin Cowdrey. Cowdrey, thinking that only top-class leg-spinners bowl googlies, didn't expect me to bowl one. So the ball pitched outside off stump and he just left it alone. But it was a vicious googly and clipped his off stump.

After my first-class cricketing days were over I toured the Cayman Islands with Fred Trueman as the captain. We played on a matting pitch where the ball would turn square, and we had this guy called Robin Hobbs who had played for England as a leg-spinner. We thought he would run through the opposition, but he bowled 10 to 15 overs without achieving anything. They were slogging him all over the place. So I asked Fred to let me have a go and I came on bowling leg-spinners and took 7 wickets for about 20 runs and we won the match easily. I was quite proud that I had achieved something that had eluded an England leg-spinner.

Two characters who stand out from Farokh's experiences of Indian domestic cricket are Raj Singh Dungarpur and the Maharajah of Vizianagram. Raj Singh is today one of the senior figures in Indian cricket, having played first-class cricket for sixteen years for the State of Rajasthan, served as a selector and on four occasions managed Indian teams on an overseas tour. He has also been president of the Indian Cricket Board. Raj Singh was never selected to the national side and put this failure down to 'complacency' which he describes as 'one of the deep rooted ills or diseases of Indian cricket'. Raj Singh was a fast medium bowler and enjoys the distinction of being the only bowler to have drawn blood from Farokh Engineer when he injured the newly selected Indian wicketkeeper on the eve of what would otherwise have been his Test debut against England in 1961. Farokh remembers him holding court at the Brabourne Stadium:

Raj Singh is a very dear friend not only of mine but of all Indian cricketers. He did a tremendous amount for cricket in India, he was extremely knowledgeable and knew records and statistics that you wouldn't even dream about. Raj was exceedingly keen about the game and was a very friendly, approachable person. He liked discussions, heated discussions held on the lawns of the CCI. That was a favourite pastime. In the evenings, many members would sit in a circle and Raj would conduct the discussions and debates on various cricketing issues. There was often keen controversy and Raj was always at the centre of it. Bhel puri and coconut water would be served by bearers all dressed in starched white cotton suits and turbans, summoned by the snap of a finger. There was music in the background and the whole atmosphere was very colonial. This practice still continues as a tradition. Whenever I visit Bombay I invariably stay at the CCI and it's wonderful. I can meet the same guys from thirty years ago and they are still engaged in the same conversation revolving around anything topical in international cricket. They all voice their opinions and if they see me or any other Test cricketer they would want to hear it from the horse's mouth – 'What do you think of this?' Raj Singh is a prince of Dungarpur, a prosperous state in beautiful Rajasthan. If Ted Dexter went on a tiger shoot it would be Raj Singh who made the arrangements and all cricketing friends always looked to Rajbai for guidance.

The Maharajkumar of Vizianagram, or 'Vizzy' as he was dubbed by Lord Hailsham in 1936, was one of the most extraordinary characters in the history of Indian cricket. He used his immense wealth, position and influence not only to sponsor the game but also to promote his position as a player. While never in possession of more than ordinary club-level cricketing skills, he plotted and intrigued to the extent that he became captain of India for their tour to England in 1936. Arriving with thirty-six items of luggage and two servants, he managed a Test average of 8.25 and dispatched home the team's outstanding all-rounder, Lala Amarnath, on disciplinary grounds. But he also received a knighthood and was an undoubted social success. Vizzy was three times elected president of the Board of Control for Cricket in India and became a member of the Indian Legislative Assembly. Farokh's memories of Vizzy were in his role as broadcaster and commentator:

Vizzy just loved the microphone and he loved the sound of his own voice. Since he was a Maharaja no one was going to tell him that he couldn't do the commentating. His favourite expression was 'ooooooooooh' and when this was broadcast on the radio, listeners used to wonder what on earth was going on, whether someone had scored a four or a six or lost a wicket, and all Vizzy could say was 'ooooooooooh' for five or six seconds. His commentating wasn't exactly the best, but he was a great character. He always used to present tiger heads or tiger skins to the captains and managers of visiting teams and someone must have remarked that he was probably a damned good shot shooting all those dangerous wild beasts. Manjrekar used to joke that during Test matches Vizzy used to hang up his transistor sets in the jungle and he was so dreadful that the tigers used to hear his commentaries and immediately drop down dead.

Apart from the Ranji and Duleep Trophies and various charity and invitation competitions, Farokh also played for the CCI and other club sides in the Dr H D Kanga Memorial League:

There is cricket in India all the year round, even during the monsoon season between July and September, which is when there is a league in Bombay, the ever popular Kanga League. Here all the Test players take part even if it is throwing it down with rain. It was a real breeding ground for experience because we played on uncovered pitches. You are talking of up to 100 clubs in Bombay divided up into divisions named after the letters in the alphabet, the divisions went up to G or H and there were so many teams – about fourteen – in each division. Polly Umrigar played for G division when in his sixties. The CCI rarely won the competition except when Kunderan, the great Vinoo Mankad, Raj Singh and myself went to play for them. But either playing for or against the CCI was a great occasion because the conditions were so superb, the facilities were marvellous. It was like playing at Lord's and was a game we very much looked forward to. The Kanga League served as a form of selection trials for the Ranji Trophy matches.

Playing domestic cricket could never have provided Farokh with the means to sustain a living, even though he continued to reside in the parental home until he got married for the first time in 1966, when he moved into his own flat. Payment for playing in the Ranji Trophy league matches was 15 rupees a day which went up to 20 rupees for the knock-out competition. Even Test cricket was not particularly remunerative: 75 rupees a day for playing in India at a time when there were 20 rupees to the English pound. When Farokh toured England for the first time the daily allowance was £1. Indian cricketers needed a day job and Farokh worked as a management trainee for Mercedes-Benz, which was controlled by TATA. Company life need not be too arduous:

When you work for a company in India you are like a professional cricketer. You are not really expected to do any serious work because you are out all the time. The average company life of the average first-class cricketer involved turning up at the office at 9.30 a.m. in a shirt and tie, signing in and then talking cricket with the bosses who were all keen on the game. 10.30 a.m. was coffee time and we would all traipse down to one of the coffee shops where a jazz trio would be playing. We drank Expresso. By the time we got back to the office it was usually time to go out for lunch and we weren't expected to come back again until the next morning. We would then go for afternoon cricket practice either for the company's team or the state team as the case may be. My role was a little different because I wanted to better myself and, while I took the afternoons off, I tried to ask for some responsible work. I was given a number of opportunities in sales and marketing. The work didn't mean direct sales to the public because the cars, trucks and buses sold themselves. It was extremely difficult buying a Mercedes car because the waiting time could be three or four years. I would deal with the sales and exports.

Working for TATA was hardly onerous, but the organisation likes having well-known sportsmen on their payroll who will perhaps continue working for the company when their playing days are over. Farokh remembers that his first salary cheque was in the order of 1,000 rupees. This enabled him to have a comfortable, though not rich, lifestyle. He didn't even own his own car until moving to England, though the family MG was often available to him. For the rest of the time he would travel short journeys by scooter. Of course there were all kinds of benefit in kind. Test cricketers were often taken out for lunch and dinner and generally offered lavish entertainment.

While domestic cricket provided Farokh with many happy memories – the camaraderie of the team and the card-playing through the night on the long train journeys – it could not satisfy his cricketing ambitions, and he was keen to make a return to the national side. The problem with playing for the best state team in India was that many of the best cricketers were on your own side. Farokh wanted to improve his batting by facing a higher class of bowler and this was rarely possible in the Ranji Trophy. Nevertheless, Farokh continued playing for Bombay on occasions even after his county cricketing commitments with Lancashire. This was possible when Farokh was selected to play for the national team playing against a touring side in India. Hence when he played in the home series against England in 1972-73 he was also able to take part in the final of the Duleep Trophy when West Zone defeated Central Zone by an innings and 172 runs.

six

Finest Hour

Farokh was finally recalled to the national team for the First Test against New Zealand to be held at the Corporation Stadium, Madras, beginning on 27 February 1965. This was to be the beginning of a two-year period during which Farokh firmly established his Test match credentials, for by the end of January 1967 his selection was more or less automatic following a glittering century made against the West Indies. Already, in the new year of 1965, Farokh had impressed with the bat in domestic games, scoring 92 against Maharashtra in a Ranji Trophy West Zone League match and 142 against Central Zone in the final of the Duleep Trophy played at the Brabourne Stadium in mid-February. The season 1964-65 was to prove Farokh's most successful with the bat and he scored 1,050 runs with an average of 47.72. Farokh returned to the Test side fired with a new passion to succeed and determined to consolidate his place. To assist him in this mission he was armed with a splendid new pair of pads purchased from Brian Bolus at the end of the England tour of 1963-64:

Now Brian Bolus was one of those batsman who played more with his pads than his bat – for some reason he thought the pad was better armoury than the bat and he would kick more balls than he would hit. I was present in the dressing room when Brian Bolus entered with his pads for sale. English leg-guards, English pads were very valuable because we couldn't get good pads at home. Bolus's left pad was like double thick, specially stuffed because he liked padding the ball, and they were specially made for him. He sold them to me for a small fortune and I spent all the pocket money that I had accumulated plus a loan from my Dad. I remember the first thing I did was to take ninety per cent of the stuffing out, the extra stuffing, because I didn't need that – I intended to hit the ball not kick it. We had the same pads for batting and wicketkeeping. Nowadays we have different pads for each, but then we couldn't afford that. We could just about afford one pair of pads. Later on they started making good cricket equipment in India and, in fact,

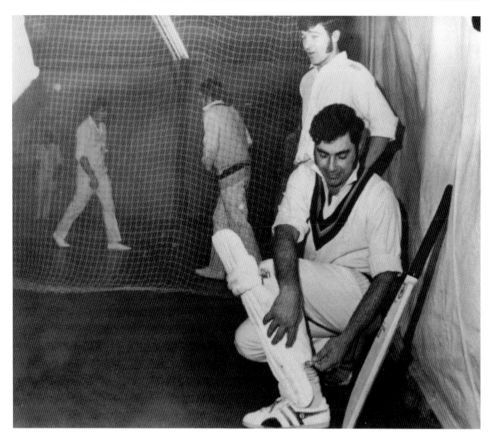

Padding up.

the majority of the cricketing leather goods that come to England is made in India.

Farokh had met a number of the current New Zealand Test players, together with John Alabaster, a number of years before during the 1955-56 New Zealand tour to India:

When I was at the late stages of school my Dad was invited for dinner at a private flat in Bombay by one of his TATA colleagues who had also invited four New Zealand Test cricketers. Now the host knew that Dr Engineer's son was very keen on cricket and that I would be simply delighted to have the opportunity of talking to four Test cricketers from the touring team so I was invited as well. I will never forget that day, for it was such a memorable experience. John Reid was there and Bert Sutcliffe and they were so nice to me, signing my autograph book 'with happy recollections'. I was so pleased and proud the next day, showing the autographs to my schoolfriends. Later on you can imagine my delight at playing a Test series against some of those guests.

Despite the fact that New Zealand were still regarded as in the second division of cricketing nations, Farokh had the greatest of respect for his opponents:

New Zealand were a very good side. They had an excellent bowling attack with quick bowlers such as Dick Collinge, Ward and Dick Motz and they were always a competitive team and fought hard. They took Test cricket very seriously indeed and they were certainly no pushover. I think they were just as good a side as the New Zealand team of today. John Reid, who captained the side, was a great man, one of the great New Zealand cricketers and now a respected member of the New Zealand Board of Control. Bert Sutcliffe was one of the finest left-handed batsmen of his time, comparing very favourably with the great Neil Harvey of Australia.

By the time of India's second series against New Zealand, India's position within international cricket had substantially improved from the time that Farokh first walked out to the crease to bat for his country in December 1961. While India had succumbed to the West Indies in 1961-62, they had not lost a series on home soil since the Australian series of 1959-60 when Richie Benaud captained the touring side. The series against England in 1963-64 had ended in a draw, as had the series against Australia in 1964-65, the first time that India had avoided a series defeat against the latter opponents. So if the New Zealanders were treated with deserved respect the Indian team still expected to win the series.

In the First Test at Madras, Farokh batted at number 9. His score of 90 was the second highest in the drawn game with Manjrekar, making 102 not out in the second innings. This was Farokh's most impressive Test innings to date and contained many of the touches of brilliance that made him such a pull with the Indian crowds. The cricket correspondent from *The Statesman*, under the headline 'Great Innings by Engineer', was generous in his praise:

> The batting soared to unexpected heights in the morning with Engineer and Nadkarni coming together for an eighth-wicket partnership of 143 achieved in 115 minutes. Quick on his feet Engineer lost no chance to score and in a display of thunder and lightening scored 90, his highest in official Test cricket. He batted for 115 minutes hitting fourteen 4s.
>
> The stand was obviously a new record for Indo-New Zealand Tests, the previous best being 33. But it was also a new record for the eighth wicket by India against any country. The previous best was 101 by the same pair against Dexter's England team in 1961…
>
> Although the morning brought about the early downfall of Borde the gay holiday crowd roared approvingly as 54 runs came forth in the first hour. It was such a welcome change to the boredom of the previous day and the man responsible for the transformation was Farokh Engineer who approached his task with a show of enterprise that could have led to poverty or riches.

Hooking viciously and driving majestically he prospered with a show of skill that knocked the heart out of the New Zealanders earlier elated by the morning's quick success...

Engineer evoked admiration by the masterly way in which he scotched everything that lifted and was particularly severe on Motz off whom he took 13 runs in one over. Neither pace nor spin seemed to make any difference to Engineer whose thundering strokes suggested that he could go on indefinitely.

As the second hour commenced Engineer was seen in his most expansive form and New Zealand had a harrowing time in the field. Soon the three hundred mark was passed a total gathered in 407 minutes and Engineer himself drove his way to 50 which, with nine devastating fours, took him 61 minutes to acquire. Nadkarni totally eclipsed by Engineer's pyrotechnics imperceptibly crept into the forties and pressed on to his 50 as a satisfying morning's play drew to a close.

The crowd, rejoicing in Nadkarni's brief emulation of his partner's panache gave the batsmen a big hand when the century partnership was completed in 78 minutes and at lunch India were in the prosperous position of 360 for seven with Engineer on 82 and Nadkarni 65.

But Engineer's cavalier innings ended ten minutes after the interval. With his sights trained on his century he mistimed a drive off Yuile and Pollard at extra cover held a brilliant tumbling catch.

In this four-day match India were all out for 397. New Zealand then replied with 315. In India's second innings the captain Pataudi waited until his side was 199 for 2 before declaring, thereby eliminating the chance of a decisive result. The Second and Third Tests also ended in draws with Farokh unable to reproduce the batting form of the First Test – he scored 10, 45, 17 and 6. His score of 17 in the Third Test at Bombay was, in fact, the second highest score of India's first innings as they collapsed to 88 all out; this was India's lowest score on home soil and they were forced to follow on for the first time against New Zealand. In the Fourth Test, played at Delhi, India won by 7 wickets, so clinching the series, but while Farokh took 3 catches he played two disappointing innings, scoring 5 and 2. Kunderan was still breathing down Farokh's neck and waiting in the wings to regain a Test place. In fact, for the Second Test, played at Calcutta, both Kunderan and Engineer were selected for the side, with Farokh keeping wicket. But after the New Zealand series Kunderan was again chosen to displace his friendly rival in the first 2 Test matches against the West Indies. It was a strange decision since Farokh was the acknowledged number one wicketkeeper and Kunderan's performance with the bat in the Second Test amounted to 36 and 12 – 7 runs short of those scored by Engineer. Farokh was soon recalled to the national side.

Farokh's captain for the New Zealand series was Nawab of Pataudi. The latter's Test match career runs parallel to that of Engineer. Both men played

46 Tests beween 1961 and 1975 with similar batting averages. Pataudi was the son of a former captain of India who had led the tour to England in 1946 and also played for England in the Bodyline Series of 1932-33. Pataudi junior took over the captaincy at the age of twenty-one following the injury to Contractor in 1962. Only a few months before this event, Pataudi was seriously injured in a car accident, almost losing the sight of his right eye; blurred vision was then the best he could hope for. He had captained Oxford University in 1961 and succeeded Dexter as captain of Sussex in 1966. Nicknamed the 'Tiger' by his father, he led India in 40 Tests, including the first overseas Test series victory against New Zealand in 1967. One of his most courageous stands was in the Melbourne Test of January 1967 when, one-eyed and one-legged, (he had sustained a pulled hamstring injury) he scored 75 and 85. Sambit Bal, writing for Wisden, considered Pataudi the 'greatest captain ever' and wrote that he 'led Indian cricket out of its morass of defeatism and instilled in his fellow cricketers a belief that winning was possible'. Farokh had the greatest admiration and respect for his captain:

I only saw Pataudi after his accident but we were both of the same era, though he was a little younger than me. Pataudi came to India with a great reputation as a county player for Sussex and apart from his batting he was renowned for his fielding. With a princely pedigree and a brilliant sporting career, he was virtually the automatic choice as captain when Contractor was forced to step down. Considering how good Pat was after his accident I can only think of what he might have been. His throws to me were deadly accurate, smack in the gloves. He had a great arm and in spite of his defective eye he played to the highest level and always very well too. People often made comparisons with Wadekar who took over as captain for a while in the early 1970s. Wadekar was certainly the luckier captain of the two but both of them knew their job and I had a good rapport and intuitive understanding with both men. The establishment liked Pat because he was a prince but they also respected him for his cricketing talents. I was very lucky to have played under a succession of great captains: Polly Umrigar, Nari Contractor, Pataudi, Wadekar and, of course, Jack Bond.

Another important member of the Indian team at this time was Chandu Borde, a right-handed batsman, leg-spin bowler and fielder excelling both in the outfield and in close up positions. His graceful, feline movements earned him the nickname 'Panther'. Borde had played a leading role in India's successful series against England in 1961-62 and perhaps reached his peak when he scored 2 centuries in 3 Tests against the West Indies in 1966-67. He captained his side in the Adelaide Test during the 1967-68 tour of Australia when Pataudi was temporarily injured. Borde played in 55 Tests and after laying down his bat continued his interest in the game as a manager and selector. Borde was another player who Farokh rated highly:

He was a very unassuming cricketer and perhaps because of that very underrated. I say this because he was a brilliant batsman, a great bowler and an absolutely fantastic cover point fielder – one of the finest fielders in India. He was also a great character, a great fighter and a most successful and respected Chairman of Selectors.

The home Test series against the West Indies began in December 1966. Captained by Sobers, the West Indies were one of the most complete teams of all time: Hunte, Bynoe, Kanhai, Butcher, Lloyd, Nurse, Hendriks, Hall, Gibbs and Griffith. This side had recently beaten the Australians 2-1 in the West Indies and England 3-1 in England. India had lost 8 of their last 10 matches against the West Indies and, while they now had batsmen able to cope with pace bowling, the prospects for this three-match series must have seemed uncertain. Farokh was reserve wicketkeeper to Kunderan for the first 2 Tests, both of which resulted in decisive wins for the West Indies.

Farokh was a witness to the extraordinary events that occurred during the Second Test at Eden Gardens, Calcutta. Motivated by both stupidity and greed, the authorities sold too many tickets. 70,000 people crowded into a stadium with accommodation for only 50,000. Following the collapse of a stand there were full-scale riots, with the police responding to crowd invasions of the pitch with batons and tear gas. The police were overwhelmed, however, and the crowd pulled up sections of turf, set fire to the stands and made straight for the rich, enclosed sections in angry pursuit of the corrupt match officials.

India v. West Indies, December 1966.

The players fled with many of the West Indies team unsure as to whether the crowd were after their heads or their autographs:

The match was cancelled for the day because of the riots. Not only were there too many people crammed into the stadium, there seemed to be about 100,000 outside the ground with what they thought were valid tickets in their hands – there was overselling, forgeries, black market exchanges, the lot. The stands were shaking and, when one of them collapsed, the two West Indies bowlers, Wes Hall and Charlie Griffith, became completely disorientated and ran through the opening created by the demolished stand. Everyone else dashed back to the pavilion and onto the team coaches to take us back to our hotel in order to avoid trouble or danger to any player. As the coach was making its way to the hotel I saw these two huge black men running down the street with a massive crowd of about 10,000 people in pursuit. But the crowd were running just to say 'Mr Hall' or 'Mr Griffith', just to touch them, more in adulation or admiration than anything else. Wes and Charlie obviously thought the crowd were out to kill them as there was such a look of terror on their faces. We took the coach as close to them as we could and I leaned out the door and shouted, 'Wes, where you going?' 'Man,' he said, 'I'm going to Dum Dum' (the name of the airport in Calcutta). 'Why?' I said, 'This lot aren't going to harm you.' As we stopped the coach I just put my hand up and the whole crowd stopped a few yards from the West Indians. 'Oh Mr Hall, Mr Hall, Mr Griffith, Mr Griffith,' they called. I said, 'Wes, they don't want to hurt you, they love you, they're admiring you, they're just being appreciative, they've never had the chance of seeing you from such close quarters before.' 'Ok, Ok, Ok,' gasped Wes and Charlie as they disappeared down the coach. To this day Wes thinks I saved his life on that occasion.

At that same match when all the players got on the team coaches, Conrad Hunte climbed the pavilion to retrieve the West Indies flag (Conrad was a man of firm principles and a member of MRA, the campaign for Moral Rearmament) and I thought that was one hell of a brave thing to do what with all the crowds throwing bricks and swarming around. But Conrad, ever the conscience of his team, had so much pride for the West Indies flag he didn't want it to come to any harm.

Not surprisingly, after this upset, the West Indies were keen to fly home and there were calls for the match to be abandoned, but after a rest day and a good deal of diplomacy play resumed. India lost the match by an innings and 45 runs.

When Farokh was selected for the Third Test to be played at Chepauk, Madras, beginning on 13 January 1967 he was on the eve of his finest hour, for his innings of 109 secured his place in the national side such that he became a regular member, excepting the tour of the West Indies in 1970-71, until his final Test match in 1975. In order to explain the dropping of Kunderan, which would have been hard to justify, the selectors put it about that he was injured when, in fact, he was not. There may have been more Machiavellian factors at work, for Farokh was chosen to open the innings at number 2. He is sure that there were elements within the selection panel who wanted an excuse to dispense with him for good. A signal failure with the bat would have provided just such an excuse, and what better way to guarantee such an outcome than to place Farokh in the unfamiliar Test opening slot against the fastest and most feared bowling attack in the world. During the previous series against New Zealand Farokh had never enjoyed a settled batting position, going from 9 to 3 to 8 to 7. Now at number 2 it was perhaps a day of reckoning. For those who may have wished to dispense with Farokh's services the plan backfired in the most spectacular fashion. The cricketing correspondent of *The Statesman* described how Farokh justified his selection

> with a sparkling century in a display of attacking batsmanship that no one present would have wanted to miss. With zeal and character he fearlessly attacked the West Indies bowling. His footwork was quick and stroke-play no less decisive.

D.J. Rutnagur of the *Daily Telegraph* wrote in similar vein:

> the ebullient Engineer, who had no reputation as an opening batsman to lose, struck four after four with either a straight drive or a smart flick to mid-wicket off the toes.

Farokh's achievement appeared all the greater since his batting partner, Sardesai, advanced his score so slowly, taking thirty-one minutes to move from 13 to 14. With regard to Farokh's hitting power and authority *The Statesman* noted how the 'spectators rubbed their eyes in disbelief' as 24 runs were added to the board in fourteen minutes. At lunch India were 125 for no loss with Engineer just six short of his century. Wisden, which summarised Farokh's innings as a 'brilliant display of controlled hitting', noted how he 'smashed a six just after the interval to bring up his hundred'. Farokh became the fourth Indian player to score a Test century against the West Indies and the second on the present tour. His partnership with Sardesai for the first wicket was a new record for India against the West Indies (the previous best was 99 by Roy and Contractor at Kanpur in 1958). Indeed it was the first century opening stand for India against the West Indies in five Test series.

The Times headline for this innings read 'Engineer flays Hall and Griffith', for the two bowlers had conceded 81 runs in their 12 overs before lunch. The *Daily Mail* assessment was that 'Engineer assault puts West Indies in danger'. Farokh had been just a whisker away from entering the record books, for no Indian batsman had yet scored a Test hundred before lunch and only three batsmen, all of them Australians, had so far scored 100 before lunch on the first day of a Test match: they were Macartney, Bradman and Trumper, the latter of whom made his century at Old Trafford. Only ten players have scored centuries before lunch on days other than the first day.

The innings undoubtedly got India off to a flying start and, aided by Borde's 125, their total reached 404. The West Indies responded with 406 but then India set the visitors a target of 322 in four and a half hours. The result was nearly a victory for India, who reduced the West Indies to 193 for 7 with still an hour and a half to go. But two critical fielding errors – Sobers being dropped twice – and Griffiths' resort to the pads and body to obstruct the ball ensured a draw. Farokh has no doubt as to the importance of this century:

That innings changed my whole life. It gave me so much prominence, so much publicity, and ensured that I was now a regular member of the India team, one of the main all-rounders of the side. My detractors, those who were gunning for me and had been silently hoping that I would fail, now had to accept that it was impossible to drop someone who had given the West Indies attack such a bloody nose. I have been reliably informed that this is the fastest Test century ever scored by an Indian, not only in terms of time but also in the number of balls faced – and this whilst opening the innings on the first morning of a Test match.

Farokh's new fame meant that commercial companies now had an additional incentive to sign him up to advertise and endorse their products:

When I first came into Test cricket I had my own autographed cricket bat. In fact, there were about fifty different manufacturers making Farokh Engineer cricket bats but you couldn't catch hold of them. They were making them all over the place and marketing them, a sort of pirating operation. But I was tied up with one particular company, Slazengers. Alan Knott and I were both contracted by Slazengers but, in my opinion, they didn't make very good cricket bats at that time. Duncan Fearnley made the best cricket bats and still does so. What we did was to scratch out the Duncan Fearnley name from their bats and put the Slazenger stickers on instead. This kept Slazenger happy when they saw what they thought were their bats being used when the film cameras showed close-ups of the batsmen. We were right at the very beginning of the whole business of endorsing cricket bats so we didn't actually see much money.

My biggest money spinner was advertising for Brylcreem. After Denis Compton I was the first person to be offered the Brylcreem contract. The product was very popular in India at one stage but sales had dipped so low that Beecham's, the manufacturers, needed a sports personality or someone flamboyant to endorse the cream. They wanted to promote flamboyance and good looks. I remember doing an advertisement with a Miss India who

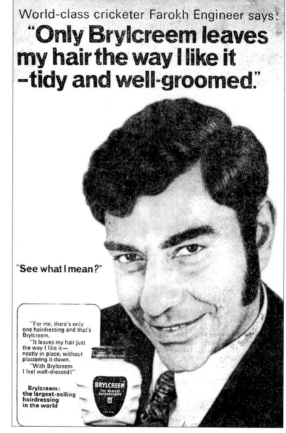

Brylcreem Boy.

was also Miss World at the time. The make-believe scenario was that a jumbo jet from Air India had just landed at Bombay Airport. A pretty young Indian girl was waiting on the runway festooned with flowers ready to greet her future husband who had just flown in from the States. The idea was that she had never met him as it was an arranged marriage. Suddenly the first class doors opened, the red carpet was rolled down and I walked down the steps. Just because or rather only because I was using Brylcreem the pretty young girl was mesmerised by my appearance and, forgetting all about her fiancé, presented me with a garland of flowers. That advertisement was incredibly successful and I became known as the 'Brylcreem Boy'. Sales were boosted and there was a tremendous growth – so much so that the following year Beecham's invited me to England to sign a contract with them. I was given a substantial sum to do a second Brylcreem advertisement and these new advertisements were all over Australia, India, the Middle East and the Far East. I was also offered a bonus to walk out of a bathroom without clothes on – except, of course, a towel draped around my waist and another around my shoulders.

Posing for the tabloids with daughter Tina.

On another occasion one of the UK tabloids made me an attractive offer to take a picture of me without my shirt on and carrying my daughter Tina on my shoulders. I thought that was a good arrangement, but there was no negotiation of contracts and no agents. We were just offered a sum. I was the first Indian Test cricketer to start advertising products. At one time it was almost embarrassing as I was endorsing five or six different goods from shaving cream to band aid. My photograph was everywhere. There was no big money, but it all added up. I might have become significantly richer if I had accepted an offer to appear in a film depicting the life of a cricketer – my dear Dad talked me out of it. He thought there would be too many temptations and distractions from the real business of cricket. Little did he know!

Farokh was now enjoying an existence on a level with stardom. He was a sought-after asset both on the sports field and in the photographer's studio. The reputation gained by his Madras century clearly whetted the appetites of a number of English county cricket clubs and it was fortuitous that the next Test series for India was to be played against England in England. There was little doubt that Farokh would be close to the top of the selectors' list. This was to be a visit that was to change the whole course of his life.

seven

A Passage to England

The 1967 Indian tour of England was held during the unusually wet first half of the summer, with matches being played between early May and mid-July. The Indian spin attack required dry, hard wickets and the English conditions dramatically reduced their effectiveness. Eight matches were played in May and India lost to both Kent and Surrey, drawing the remaining fixtures. In June, India beat Cambridge University and Derbyshire but lost the first 2 Tests played at Headingley and Lord's. The remaining two fixtures, including a match against Lancashire at Southport, were drawn. In July the results were even more depressing, with defeats by Yorkshire and Leicestershire, a draw against Nottinghamshire and a defeat in the final Test at Edgbaston. Farokh clocked up 5 half centuries during the tour, his most successful performance being in the First Test where he scored 42 and 87. Before a disappointingly small crowd, on account of India's poor performances, England made 550 for 4 declared with Boycott not out on 246, a slow scoring feat for which he was dropped in the Second Test. In India's reply Farokh was one of only three batsmen to enter double figures and the side collapsed to 164. India were forced to follow on and made a spirited fightback, scoring 510, only the second occasion in Test match history that a side had passed 500 in the follow on, the other two instances being when England made 551 at Trent Bridge against South Africa in 1947 and when Pakistan made 647 for 8 at Bridgetown against the West Indies in 1958. In reference to Farokh's innings, Wisden recorded:

> Surti… went in first with Engineer but soon edged Snow to the wicket-keeper. Then the England bowlers sampled the brilliant form Indian batsmen often display on their own sun drenched grounds.
>
> In a scintillating record second-wicket stand of 168 for India against England in two and a half hours, Engineer and Wadekar struck boundary after boundary.
>
> Engineer hit fourteen 4s and after he left, Wadekar turned to defence…

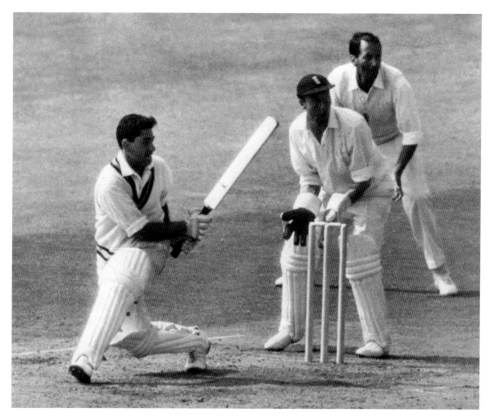

England v. India, 1967 – no helmets please.

Pride had been restored, but little could truly disguise the disappointing progress of the tour. The Indian team was demoralised by the weather, injuries, inadequate clothing and equipment, inappropriate food for the vegetarians and a parsimonious daily allowance. From Farokh's personal point of view, however, it was a tour full of opportunities for securing his cricketing future:

When I came to England in 1967, the thought of playing county cricket had not even crossed my mind. I had a demanding job in India working for Mercedes-Benz and my ambitions were to continue in their employment while developing my cricket interests in the afternoons, evenings and weekends. The first person to plant the seed of the idea of playing county cricket was John Arlott – one of the greatest commentators of all time, with only Brian Johnston as a close rival. John was kind enough to invite me to his house in Hampshire, where he plied me with Beaujolais and then said, 'Farokh, you should be playing county cricket, you'd be very popular here.' A short time after this, Syd Buller, one of the greatest umpires England has ever produced, almost echoed the words of John Arlott. The two men had obviously been talking and were very keen on the idea of Hampshire offering me a contract. I just shrugged my shoulders after these approaches, I couldn't even imagine playing cricket seven days a week. I thought to myself that cricket is meant for fun, it's not a job. But I couldn't help beginning to turn the suggestion over in my mind. Somehow it got into the papers that Hampshire was interested and this led to Don Kenyon, the Chairman of Worcestershire and Chairman of the English Selectors, approaching me on behalf of his county. 'Farokh,' he said, 'I hear you may be interested in playing county cricket.' 'I certainly am not,' I replied. 'But it's in the papers that Hampshire have offered you a contract.' I had to explain to him that while Hampshire had honoured me with their interest, I hadn't even promised to think about it as I was aware that if my employers got to hear about all this they would certainly take a dim view of the fact that I hadn't so much as spoken to them about any intention of coming to England. Before I could think about things any further, Somerset joined Hampshire and Worcestershire in courting my services. Somerset made me a very lucrative offer and to cap it all, when we came to play against Lancashire at Southport, they too expressed an interest. Lancashire promised to top all the other offers, but I had to explain to them that I didn't have an agent and that I hadn't discussed any financial terms with any of the other counties. I did, however, give Lancashire an undertaking that when I returned to India I would consult with TATA (they controlled Mercedes-Benz in India) and see if they would give me leave for six months to come and play county cricket. By this time I was beginning to get really quite keen on the idea. It was certainly a great opportunity, for England was the only country in the world where it was possible to play professional cricket. I could see that no player could be considered complete until he had experienced county cricket where you play on different wickets almost every day, under different conditions, on uncovered pitches and against some of the finest bowlers in the world. I could see that this would be a golden way of taking my cricket a further stage forward.

The three-day match between India and Lancashire at Southport took place on 3-5 June. Lancashire batted first and were all out for 197. Farokh then opened the Indian innings with Kunderan, scoring 16 in a total of 184. Lancashire then replied with 186 for 8 declared and Farokh made the second highest Indian score of 38 in his second innings. The game ended in a draw. In addition to his contribution with the bat, Farokh took 3 catches, dismissing Pullar to the pavilion twice, together with Pilling. Farokh still remembers this occasion:

We were actually a bit disappointed that the game wasn't played at the famous Old Trafford Test ground. But Southport was a delightful seaside resort with, so we were reliably informed, more Rolls Royces per square mile than anywhere else in the country. It was a great atmosphere, with champagne flowing in the marquees and a brass band playing to the capacity crowd. One of the boundaries at Southport is a little short because the railway line runs next to the ground. I opened the batting in both innings and this rather quick bowler came on from one end and started bowling a bit short of a length. I hit him quite a few times onto the railway line and it was only afterwards that I realised that this was the great Brian Statham. In fact, Lancashire had offered me a contract before they saw me tearing into their prized bowler but maybe my shots did something to seal the matter.

Not only was Farokh an Anglophile on account of his Parsee and family background, but he had developed a positive liking for the country during his first visit in 1962 when he had stopped off for a stay with his brother, Darius, after taking part in the tour to the West Indies:

Darius lived in Edgware, London. I was immediately struck by the greenery of the country. I came to love the English way of life and the coolness of the climate. I must be the only person in England who likes the English weather – okay, it rains from time to time, but the sun shines after that. I'm quite relaxed about it, no big deal. I saw a few of the county games and was very impressed with the crowds and the structure of the game over here. I didn't really get much beyond London as I didn't have the money to travel. On Sunday mornings I used to play tennis with my brother and boy did I work up an appetite. I was so hungry after the game and as we walked back to Darius' house I could smell the Sunday roasts cooking in the ovens of the houses along the way. I just couldn't wait to tuck into my food.

But if Farokh had developed a liking for England then it was traditional England, the England of the southern counties: tennis, Sunday roasts and pints of warm ale. The industrial north with its squalor and drizzle was a far cry from the rural attractions of Hampshire, Worcestershire and Somerset. Yet Lancashire must have had counter-attractions:

Somehow Lancashire seemed to me to be a great county, a great club, a great membership and great people. I had heard that the people in the north were a lot friendlier than those in the south and, though I had some cracking friends in the south, how true that turned out to be. By and large the Lancashire folk are lovely people, very, very genuine. They took me to their hearts and I took them very much to heart also. My wife, Julie, is a Lancastrian. I've always seemed to have a good rapport, a good understanding with Lancashire people and they always supported me. One incident in particular stands out in my mind to illustrate this: I had just played an important part in beating England in a Test match at The Oval and the very next day I was playing in a county game at Old Trafford; I was a little uncertain as to what kind of reception I would get, but when I walked down the steps to bat everyone in the members enclosure and everyone else stood up and gave me tremendous applause; it was a standing ovation that really touched my heart. I had a lump in my throat and tears in my eyes, for here were a crowd of Englishmen and women but, just as important, they were also Lancastrians and as such they were proud of my achievement.

While Lancashire was interested in signing up Farokh they also had their eyes on Garry Sobers:

In the late 1960s, county cricket was very much in need of a shot in the arm to increase attendances, boost revenues and get sponsors. The clubs wanted attractive and entertaining players from all over the world and they also wanted big names. Sobers was Lancashire's first choice and he was to be offered a special registration which meant that he would be able to play for the club immediately. There was a rule that one foreign player could be given this special registration while the other had to qualify. Initially I thought I would have to qualify by playing in the Lancashire League for a year or living in Lancashire. But Lancashire and Sobers were unable to agree on financial terms so I was offered the special registration which, of course, I jumped at. At that time there was a relatively small number of foreign players in the county game: Sobers, Kanhai, Mike Procter, Barry Richards and myself. Although there had been foreign players before in the English game, such as Ken Grieves, we were the first foreign players to be offered medium-term contracts – Lancashire signed me up for three years. We were soon to be followed by such great players as Clive Lloyd, Gordon Greenidge, Desmond Haynes, Malcolm Marshal, Barry Richards, Lance Gibbs and many others. I am delighted to see that today many Indian players are appreciating the benefits of playing county cricket in England – the 2003 season sees Virender Sehwag at Leicestershire, Yuvraj Singh at Yorkshire and Harbhajan Singh at Lancashire.

Despite the excitement surrounding the prospect of playing for Lancashire, Farokh's immediate task in the middle of the summer of 1967 was to prepare himself for two major foreign tours, and of course what could be a tricky set of negotiations with his Indian employers. On their journey back from England the Indian party made a goodwill stopover in East Africa, principally as a concession to the immigrant Indian population, and in a match at Kampala on 19 August Farokh scored an aggregate of 103. The generosity of the wealthy hosts took the form of the liberal dispensing of scotch and champagne at the various garden parties and other functions. Farokh, who liked just a small scotch with plenty of soda, remembers being obliged to toss the excess alcohol into the bushes when the hosts' backs were turned. Drink has never been one of his vices. Almost as soon as the Indian team reached home they began preparing for their first away tour of Australia for twenty years.

In many ways the Australian tour of 1967-68 was an unmitigated disaster. India failed to win a single first-class game. Yet as the series progressed there were clear signs of improvement and India lost the Third Test by only 39 runs. Once again India were plagued by injury and their captain, Pataudi, was unable to play in the First Test while Chandra had to return home after playing in the first 2 Tests. For Farokh the tour began well and he scored 128 in the first innings of the first match against Western Australia at Perth on 25 November, but India still lost the game. They also lost the next match against South Australia at Adelaide with Farokh scoring 37 and 48. In the First Test at Adelaide Oval, Australia scored 335 in their first innings after winning the toss. India replied with 307, Engineer scoring 89 – both the highest Indian score of the innings and Farokh's highest score in the Test series. Cited in *The Statesman*, Frank Tyson wrote of this achievement:

> Before a crowd reminiscent of 'the deserted village' the spirit of village cricket yesterday returned to the Test match sphere on the second day. It was personified in one Farokh Engineer who in under two hours played an innings of 89 as only he can and one suspects in the only way he knows.
>
> With the frequent help of the fortunate inside edge he hammered home to the Australian bowlers the inadvisability of bowling on his leg stump – a lesson which he occasionally interspersed with a classical cover-drive.

Centuries by both Simpson and Cowper in Australia's second innings helped them to win by a comfortable margin of 146 runs. When Farokh lost his wicket after being run out in the second innings, he went to the dressing room to find Sir Donald Bradman waiting for him:

India in Australia, 1967-68.

Sir Donald had been watching the game and noticed that I was playing in rubber-soled shoes. I preferred this footwear, since cricket boots were not as comfortable as they are today. But Sir Don regarded this as completely unacceptable and gave me the greatest roasting I have ever received in a dressing room. I tried to explain, but he wouldn't listen and absolutely chewed me up. I kept wondering to myself, 'Why is he doing this? What am I to him?' and eventually began to take it all as something of a compliment. After ten minutes or so of this treatment, Sir Don completely changed his tune and asked whether I would be free for the evening. He arranged to pick me up from Hotel Australia and drove me to his home where I was served with carrot juice and a vegetarian meal before being entertained to a slide-show of Sir Don's cricket and other sporting exploits. His commentary was full of remarks such as, 'Look at that ball pitched on the off stump but still I hit it to square leg'. I was in a permanent state of amazement that Sir Don should be taking so much time with me and thought to myself what a fortunate man I was to be given such a treat in the heart of Sir Don's home. From that time onwards until he passed away, one of the first cards to arrive every Christmas was from Sir Don and Lady Bradman.

Only one day separated the First from the Second Test at Melbourne, beginning on 30 December. This time India won the toss and decided to bat. At one point the score was 25 for 5 and the side was all out for 173 with only the injured Pataudi reaching a half century. Farokh was dispatched for 9. In the Australian reply of 529, Simpson, Lawry and Chappell made centuries. India fared better in their second innings, scoring 352 with Farokh making 42, but the principal consolation of the innings and 4 runs defeat was the fearless performance of the lame and one-eyed Pataudi who was praised by Wisden for combining 'batting genius with courage'. In the words of Mihir Bose he 'once

With Borde and The Don at Melbourne, January 1968.

again gave the battered Indian psyche a lift'. Farokh did not play in the drawn match against New South Wales in early January 1968, and the game against Queensland was abandoned. The Third and Fourth Tests were, as with the First and Second, back to back. In the former game Farokh failed to impress with the bat, but he made 17 and 37 in the final Test when Australia won by 144 runs. Summarising Farokh's contribution to this series, Wisden wrote:

> Engineer always looked an exciting, if venturesome opener; he scored a fine century against Western Australia and he played other good innings, but too often he fell to a rash stroke.

The Australian tour was immediately followed by a four Test match series against New Zealand. This was to be Farokh's most successful overseas tour to date with the bat and he averaged just over 40. It was also to be India's most successful overseas tour and they won three of the Tests, so winning their first overseas series. In the First Test at Carisbrook, Dunedin, India won by 5 wickets and Farokh scored 63 and 29. According to *The Statesman*, Engineer and Abid Ali began India's second innings 'in a blaze of runs' and took 30 runs off the first 4 overs in thirteen minutes. Perhaps the elation surrounding this victory led to overconfidence, for in the Second Test at Lancaster Park, Christchurch, India won the toss, decided to field and let New Zealand score 502, with the captain, Graham Dowling, making 239 before he was stumped by Engineer off the bowling of Prasanna. India then batted badly and were 50 for 3, all out for 288 and forced to follow on. Farokh was then dropped in the slips by Burgess when he was on 8, but went on to make 63 for the second time in the series, the highest score of the Indian second innings. New Zealand won the match by 6 wickets. In the Third test at Basin Reserve, Wellington, Farokh made his contribution to restricting the New Zealanders to 186 by taking 2 catches and stumping Taylor. In the Indian first innings he was run out after making 44, including 7 fours, the second highest score in a total of 327. New Zealand were again bowled out for under 200 and India won the match by 8 wickets. The Fourth and final Test took place at Eden Park, Auckland. After India were 13 for 2, *The Statesman* records that 'Engineer took charge and gave a delightful display of attacking batting... he was in superb form'. For the third time in the series Farokh fell victim to the bowling of Motz when he was on 44. In reply to India's total of 252, New Zealand managed 140, losing both openers, Dowling and Murray, to catches by Engineer off the bowling of Surti. In their second innings, India declared at 261 for 5 wickets, Farokh scoring 48, and the match was won by the impressive margin of 272 runs. So the series was won and Farokh was able to return home in order to make final preparations for his new life in England.

TATA, Farokh's employers, had been more than selfless and generous in their response to Farokh's ideas for moving to England for three years. They both encouraged him to accept the Lancashire offer and promised to hold his management job open for him when he returned. This gave Farokh the security to proceed in the knowledge that, should things not work out favourably for him, he had guaranteed employment back home. But Farokh was also proposing to move to a country where his closest family friend, his brother, was resident, and Darius had been extremely encouraging when he first heard about the various contract offers:

Darius was a major influence in my decision to come to England. He told me that the cricket was wonderful and more challenging and competitive than in India and that during the summer some of the best batsmen in the world along with the best bowlers and fielders were playing in England. He stressed that I would be making cricket a profession, playing for seven days a week, for six months of the year and getting paid for it. He said I would love it.

My father, on the other hand, left the decision entirely to me. He asked me to do what I thought best. He didn't try to persuade me one way or the other. Although we would be a great distance apart, he promised to spend the summers in England. My father became quite a regular feature at Old Trafford. He still loved to see me playing cricket and rarely missed a home county game.

There was also the fact that I was becoming increasingly cheesed off with the cricketing politics that went on in India. I wanted to get away from an environment where you had to lick people's backsides in order to get somewhere. I was simply not cut out for that kind of thing.

Not everyone from the Indian community in India could understand Farokh's decision to transfer his cricketing career to the mother country, given the kudos he enjoyed at home:

I was certainly the toast of India, advertising for Brylcreem, for Johnson & Johnson – you name it and I was advertising the product. I was on every billboard, in every advertising brochure; I was the name in Indian cricket until Gavaskar came on the scene. Whenever there was a modelling contract I was given the first refusal and when I didn't want it the others picked up the scraps. Somebody once said to me, 'Farokh, you have India at your feet, you are the king. Why did you decide to go to England and become a second-class citizen?' Well, I nearly laughed in his face, because at that time I had just been invited to judge the Miss UK competition in England – hardly a bad thing for a second-class citizen to be involved with. I'd had hot dinners at Buckingham Palace, drinks with Prime Ministers, meetings with showbiz people and celebrities from the world of pop, I became friendly with Mick Jagger and would go backstage with the Rolling Stones during their concerts. Cliff Richard, Bryan Ferry, Tim Rice, The Beatles, The Bee Gees... these were household names that I never thought I would meet and there's this guy asking why I went to England to live the life of a second-class citizen. I told him, 'I'm anything but a second-class citizen, pal'.

Certainly Farokh was given the warmest of receptions when he first arrived in Lancashire:

Lancashire County Cricket Club found me a house in Timperley, a suburb in south Manchester near Altrincham. When I arrived at Ringway Airport with my family, Rose Fitzgibbon from the club came to pick us up in her car (Rose later became the first lady cricket secretary of Lancashire – a job she carried out with great aplomb and distinction). It was getting late in the day and it was bitterly cold. All the neighbours from the street I was going to live in had heard that I was coming and they erected this massive sign saying something like 'Welcome to Lancashire, Farokh'. It was certainly a heartwarming sight and all the neighbours came to say hello and one of them helped me to light a coal fire in the house – this was the first time I had lit a house fire but it was definitely needed! They used to take me to the pub to show me off, introducing me as a neighbour. Then another one would shout, 'No he's not, he's my neighbour', and so it would go on. Their friendliness was wonderful. Every time I had a success at Old Trafford or in an away ground, they would be standing at their gates on my return: 'Well done Farokh Engineer,' they would shout, 'Well done Farokh.'

In addition to arranging suitable accommodation for Farokh and his family, Lancashire CCC supplied him with a car. But first he had to pass a British driving test:

I had been driving a car in Bombay and if you can drive a car there you can drive a car anywhere in the world. You do everything wrong – zig-zagging in and out, an eye for the gap, first off from the traffic lights, like a centre-forward weaving his way down the pitch to score a goal. That's how you drive in Bombay. On the day of my test it was warm and sunny. I was dressed in a short-sleeved shirt and the windows were down. Along comes this posh, old-fashioned gentleman in his immaculate suit. He sat down next to me and asked me to start up the engine. I was so confident, the radio was on, I felt I had good control. I had one hand on the steering wheel, the other outside the window, whistling to the radio music – just like one does in Bombay. I thought it was just a formality. I was there to show him how good I was – I didn't even pay attention to the speed limit. At the end of the test the examiner said, 'Mr Engineer, I do not doubt your driving ability, in fact, you are a very good driver, but have you ever read the Highway Code?' I had never heard of it and asked what it was. The examiner produced a little book from his pocket and said, 'Normally when we fail someone they have to reapply and it's a long drawn-out process. But in your case if you can

Baby you can drive my car.

read the Highway Code and come and see me again next week we will take it from there.' I was really dejected having failed my driving test, but I read his little book and when I went to see the examiner again he waved me through.

My first car was a red Ford Escort. It had to be red because of the red rose of the county. It was obtained from Quick's, who did a special deal with the club – it wasn't exactly a sponsored car but a car that I got for my own use. The very first morning when I was driving down to Old Trafford I was going through Stretford. The traffic lights ahead were green and there was a car in front of me. At the same time there was an interesting and curvacious blonde walking on the left-hand side of the road. Now you don't see that many blondes in Bombay, so I took my eye off the driving (as any self-respecting man would do) to have a good look at her, admiring her figure and so forth. But to my horror, the car in front suddenly braked for no apparent reason (the driver later claimed that a dog had run in front of him) and because of the wet road surface I skidded into his boot. I was so embarrassed (the photograph of me receiving the keys to the car hadn't yet been published in the Manchester Evening News*) but when I told the story to*

Norman Quick, the head of the company, he couldn't stop laughing and assured me that the insurance would look after everything and he arranged for me to take another car. I promised myself that that would be the last time a blonde got me into trouble – and how very wrong I was.

Even though Farokh's arrival in England almost exactly coincided with Enoch Powell's 'Rivers of Blood' speeches, he encountered virtually no racism in his adopted country:

This was possibly because of the colour of my skin, which is lighter than that of many Indians. Many people who don't know me can't even guess that I'm from India. They probably take me for an Italian or Greek or some other continental – it's not until I open my mouth and start shaking my neck that they realise. The complete or almost complete lack of any racist sentiment towards me was clearly demonstrated in 1976 when I had my benefit year. I had the highest benefit for Lancashire. It was a record within the first three months. From the sale of the brochure alone I made £10,000 and the previous single record had been that of Cyril Washbrook more than twenty-five years before. I changed the possibilities of what a benefit could achieve. I remember we had a Caribbean evening where the tickets were £5 a head and Cedric Rhoades came down on me like a ton of bricks claiming that Lancashire members could never afford £5 a head. But the event was a great success. I have been fortunate in that I've virtually never encountered opposition because of the colour of my skin.

There is one tale of Farokh encountering a less than friendly reception at a Roses match played at Headingley. Both Farokh and Clive Lloyd were warned that hostility from certain sections of the crowd was more than a possibility. David Lloyd tells the story that as soon as the Lancashire team had deposited their kit in the dressing room, they would stand on the balcony and look out towards the popular side of the ground. Every year there would be one chap sitting on his own with nobody within 20 yards of him. He was the instigator of the barracking. On this occasion he was there again, attired in bib and braces, boiler suit and flat cap with a lunch box on his knee. As Lancashire walked onto the field this character boomed across the ground: 'Here they come, the League of Nations, they're all shapes, colours and sizes, this lot, and what's that at back of t'stumps, he's not fro' Wigan'.

On another occasion the tables were turned by Farokh himself as related by M.H. Stevenson:

> Some time ago Peter Lever had bowled superbly well at Lord's to win a hard-fought match for Lancashire. Sir Neville Cardus came into the Lancashire dressing-room to congratulate him. 'I'm sure,' said Sir Neville, 'that you must be proud today to be a Lancastrian.'

'Nay,' said Lever, 'I was born in Todmorden. That's in Yorkshire, Sir Neville.'
And a voice from behind them, that of Farokh Engineer, muttered darkly:
'Bloody foreigner!'

Professional cricket-playing for Lancashire would only occupy Farokh between April and September. With a young family to support he needed to think of ways of earning a living over the winter months. After several years' experience as a management trainee working for Mercedes-Benz in Bombay, Farokh was anxious to develop his business skills, especially in the field of sales and marketing:

When I arrived in Lancashire I asked if they could put me in touch with some enterprise that might offer a similar management traineeship to the one I had enjoyed with TATA. It just so happened that Macgregor Smith, the Financial Controller of Hawker Siddeley, was on friendly terms with the Lancashire chairman. For a Scotsman, Macgregor Smith was a mad-keen Lancashire supporter and he gave me a job opportunity to work at their base in Chadderton, which is in north Manchester. I have to say that I hated every minute of it, at least to begin with. I had to leave my house at 6 a.m. every morning when it was often dark, cold and gloomy so that I arrived at the firm in time to clock in with my card. I used to detest that because if you were late, you were pulled up and asked to account for your lateness. It certainly wasn't like working for TATA when, as a cricketer, I could turn up more or less when I liked provided I signed in the book – the set up in India was very much more relaxed. At Hawker Siddeley there was a strict business regime and insistence upon punctuality – never my strong point. But I'm sure it was all great for my character and I learnt a lot from the different management jobs I was given. I was moved around the departments and aviation is something I love because of my piloting experience. When I got used to the discipline I enjoyed it immensely but I never got used to those early morning starts. I recall working in Organisation and Methods, O & M, and OR, Operational Research. Whenever something went wrong in one of the departments (not something technical for although I'm Engineer by name I can't even change a plug with a screwdriver), something administrative, we would be sent in to try to improve that department and more often than not the members of the department would suggest the ideas for improvement. We had to interview them and write out reports and discuss why it took so long to do a particular job, why six men were doing a job that could be done by two and so on. The unions didn't take kindly to what we were doing for obvious reasons. The pay was peanuts but it was the experience that mattered.

Farokh soon settled into Manchester life. He would often go to watch Manchester United and Manchester City play during the football season and gradually got used to the geography of the city and the country. He soon mastered the route to Old Trafford, but it could be a different story when it came to away games:

On one occasion I was driving to Southport with Clive Lloyd. Not for the first time we lost our way – neither Clive nor myself are the best of navigators. We knew things were serious when on one of the highways we passed other members of the team going in the opposite direction. I applied the brakes, did a U-turn and eventually arrived at the ground with minutes to spare before the match.

He was also known for placing excessive reliance on the M6, which was fine for the majority of counties but less than helpful when Lancashire played Yorkshire at Headingley. When Ken Snellgrove, Lancashire's Scouse batsman, mischievously encouraged Farokh to find the way down his favourite motorway, the forty-minute journey from Manchester to Leeds took him four hours.

Again, according to David Lloyd, comedians used to tell a joke about Farokh concerning the time when his car was in for a service and he had to catch a bus back home. He asked his team-mates how he would know which bus to get on and was told to ask for the destination indicated on the front of the bus. When the bus came along, Farokh asked for 'one to Leyland Motors'. The driver replied, 'We don't go to Leyland Motors, pal. This is the Altrincham run.' 'It says Leyland Motors on the front of the bus,' said Farokh. The driver replied, 'Aye, and it says India on the tyres but we're not taking you home!'

Another gag about Farokh concerns a round of golf he was enjoying with Bobby Charlton. Farokh himself takes up the story:

On the point of my making a crucial putt Bobby remarked, 'Hey Rookie, isn't there a war going on between your country and Pakistan?' 'Yes, Bobby', I replied. Bobby, obviously trying to distract me from lining up the putt mischievously continued, 'Haven't you thought of going back home to help your countrymen out?' 'Of course, Bobby,' I said, 'I'll go when the fighting gets nearer my village.' At which stage Bobby asked, 'Which bloody village?' I smiled, stroked my putt and replied, 'Altrincham, mate.'

All these stories suggest that Farokh soon became an adopted son of Lancashire. He regarded himself as one of the Lancashire folk and the feelings were fully reciprocated. He was going to help put Lancashire County Cricket Club back on the map, to help restore pride and success to the club and fill the cabinets with trophies and silverware. Farokh was soon providing laughter and an infectious enthusiasm for the task ahead. It was little surprise that Lancashire soon regarded him as one of their own.

eight

The Red Rose

Established in 1864, Lancashire County Cricket Club had a fine ground, a number of legendary players to its credit and an illustrious history. Old Trafford cricket ground dates from 1857 when Manchester Cricket Club rented the site from Sir Humphrey De Trafford, having been obliged to move from their original location, less than a mile away on the Chester Road, to make way for the Manchester Art Treasures Exhibition. The original light and elegant pavilion faced with glass and timber made way for a grand stone-built Victorian structure designed by Muirhead which was complete for the beginning of the 1895 season. Facilities included a conventional long room on the ground floor, committee and dressing rooms on the first floor and a roof balcony with covered seats for club members. The one-time England captain, president of the MCC, under-secretary for India and governor of Bombay, Lord Harris, described the Old Trafford Cricket Ground as the best in the country. In 1884, it became only the second ground after The Oval to stage Test cricket in England when it was host to the touring Australians; the England side was captained by A.N. Hornby, the Lancashire captain, and included three other Lancashire players – Dick Barlow, Allan Steel and Richard Pilling. W.G. Grace opened the batting and the three-day match was eventually drawn. From that point onwards Old Trafford became associated with a host of memorable cricketing occasions, some of which had an Indian connection. Certainly the earliest was when K.S. Ranjitsinhji, the first Indian to play Test cricket, made 154 not out for England, including 100 before lunch, in their second innings against Australia after they had been forced to follow on in the Second Test of July 1896. While Australia still won the match by 3 wickets, Ranji's innings was described by the Australian all-rounder George Giffen as 'absolutely the finest innings I have seen' and he called Ranji 'the batting wonder of the age'. Wisden used similar terms of praise: 'It is safe to say that a finer or more finished display has never been seen on a great occasion'. Forty years later Walter Hammond's 167 in England's first innings against India inspired expressions of gratitude from the admiring opponents who proclaimed themselves privileged to have been both the means and the witness to the glorious achievement. On the second day of the same match, more runs were scored by England and India together than on any Test match day before or since. A less happy occasion for the Indian tourists came in July 1952 when Freddie Trueman's 8 for 31 blew them away for 58, the lowest Test score made on the ground. Bedser's 5 for 27 helped dispatch India for 82 in their second innings and England won by an innings and 207 runs. Four years later Jim Laker entered the record books when he took 10 for 53 against Australia, the first time 10 wickets had been taken in Test cricket. In the first innings Laker's figures were 9 for 37 so he also broke the record for the aggregate number of wickets in a Test match, which had previously stood at 17. It took Farokh little time to fall under the charms of his new ground:

It was a second home to me, it was home from home in every sense of the word and from day one the Lancashire Committee, my team-mates, the fans, the members, everyone there made me feel so very welcome and part of the set-up – I'm glad to say that whenever I go to Old Trafford I feel I'm at my ground. I knew virtually every blade of grass there. Even Julius the worm used to pop up and say hello – I used to tell him to get back under the ground before someone trod on him!

I think Old Trafford has a great pitch and superb facilities for both home and away teams. Some might argue that the ground should be straight ahead rather than alongside the pavilion so the members can watch what the bowler is doing. This would be the normal arrangement, though Lord's is an exception – at The Oval the pavilion is at an angle. Whenever Martin Edwards, the Manchester United chairman, visited Old Trafford, he never sat in the Committee Room with the bigwigs but exactly behind the bowler's arm. The faciltities were very good even in 1968 and they compared very favourably with those at the Brabourne Stadium. The players' dressing rooms are in one corner of the pavilion along with the players' balcony – one for each side. This is exactly what you want so there is some privacy. There was a players' dining room and the food was really quite good, though it could get a bit monotonous – not enough curries. To one side of the main pavilion was a separate ladies' pavilion – men were allowed in there as guests and players were free to go and sit with their families – but in later years common sense prevailed and I for one was delighted that ladies were made welcome in the main pavilion; this was not the case during my playing days.

Old Trafford was steeped in tradition and you were always aware of the proud history as you wandered down the long room which was lined with photographs, or visited the library or Committee Room. You always knew that the greats of time past had walked through this room or up these steps,

Not one from the coaching manual.

and I remember overhearing conversations about the Tyldesley brothers or Eddie Paynter and so on. I felt privileged to be playing where these legends had played.

The wicket was a good sporting wicket. You were never really 'in' at Old Trafford, for you could always receive a vicious delivery, the ball doing what the bowler put into it – it rewarded effort. Apart from the ground itself there was an indoor school with inside nets and squash courts. After or before cricket practice I used to go down to the squash courts with Clive Lloyd. We were both keen players. We used to think that a vigorous game of squash would sharpen our reflexes on the eve of a game.

Old Trafford was just a superb place to be. In 1968 it can't have been so different from the beginning of the century, as the hospitality boxes were yet to come. The pavilion was the centre of the ground with the stadium all around it.

Lancashire's most successful winning spree before the First World War came in the quarter century between 1879 and 1904. Principally under the captaincies of A.N. Hornby and Archie Maclaren, Lancashire won the County Championship outright on three occasions – in 1881, 1897 and 1904 – and were joint champions on another three occasions – in 1879, 1882 and 1889. Furthermore, in 1888, a strong Lancashire side beat the Australian tourists at Old Trafford, with the Lancashire and England left-arm spin bowler Johnny Briggs taking 4 for 34 and 5 for 15 – Briggs remains the only cricketer to have taken a Test hat-trick and scored a century for England. The most oustanding talent of this era was undoubtedly the Harrow-educated Archie Maclaren. Neville Cardus wrote that 'his cricket belonged in the golden age of the game, to the spacious and opulent England of his day'. He played for the county between 1890 and 1914, scoring a century against Sussex at Hove on his debut at the age of eighteen. In 1894 Maclaren became the Lancashire captain in succession to Hornby, and was soon surrounded by players of exceptional quality, as was recognised by the England selectors, who picked S.F. Barnes, R.H. Spooner, J.T. Tyldesley and Walter Brearly. In the following year Maclaren broke W.G. Grace's first-class record of 344 by scoring 424 against Somerset at Taunton; this record stood until February 1923 when W.H. Ponsford made 429 for Victoria against Tasmania. So far only seven batsmen, including Bradman and Brian Lara, have bettered Maclaren's score. Maclaren played in 35 Tests scoring 5 centuries and 8 half-centuries and captained England in 22 matches between 1897 and 1909. Wisden described him as an 'immaculate batsman possessing the grand manner' and considered his championship season of 1904, when his side remained undefeated, as 'the brightest in the history of Lancashire cricket'.

In the inter-war years Lancashire's greatest success occurred in the decade beginning with their Diamond Jubilee season of 1924. In that year they inflicted their greatest humiliation on Yorkshire in the Roses match, bowling them out for 33 when they needed only 57 to win. It was said that the whole of Yorkshire was struck silent by the result! Major Leonard Green was appointed captain in 1926 and led Lancashire to a hat-trick of championships. Some claim that this championship side was the best that Lancashire ever produced, containing such legendary names as the Australian fast bowler Ted McDonald and the former England batsman Harry Makepeace, together with four current England players – the wicketkeeper George Duckworth, spin bowler Richard Tyldesley and batsmen Charles Hallows and Ernest Tyldesley. Ernest Tyldesley's career for Lancashire stretched between 1909 and 1936. He played more matches and scored more runs for the county than any other player. According to Graham Holburn, 'Like good wine, he improved with age'. He had to wait until he was thirty-two before playing for England and won the last of his 14 caps when he was forty with a Test batting average of 55. In 1934 he struck his hundredth first-class century. Neville Cardus wrote in 1932, 'He is never a vulgar or blatant batsman; even when he drives or pulls

Right: Captain Hook.

Below: Quick as a flash.

strongly there is a certain courtesy in his play, the poise of taste and discretion.' The County Championship was won again in 1930 and 1934 under the captaincy of P.T. Eckersley, but after this, Lancashire's fortunes appeared to falter. The promise of a young reconstructed side failed to materialise in the late 1930s in the face of wet weather and the drift to war.

The successes of the post-war years when Lancashire became joint champions in 1950, runners-up in 1956 and third placed in 1946, 1947 and 1951-53 were largely due to the opening partnership of Washbrook and Winston Place, who both exceeded 2,500 runs in 1947 and scored 19 centuries between them. Cyril Washbrook was Lancashire's finest player in the post-war era. He first played for the county in 1933 and at nineteen was the youngest Lancastrian to score a first-class century with 152 in his second match. He captained the side from 1954 to 1959, Lancashire's first professional captain. At Test level for England he played in 37 matches, scoring over 2,500 runs and averaging over 42. His name is often linked with that of Len Hutton, for together they established a successful opening partnership for England, forging three successive century partnerships against Australia in 1946-47 and, in the following season, hitting 359 against South Africa at Johannesburg, still an English Test record. One of his most famous innings was when, after a six-year gap, he was recalled to the England side at the age of forty-two to face the Australians at Headingley. He came in to bat with England 17 for 3 and then shared a 187-run partnership with Peter May, finally falling victim to Richie Benaud when on 98. Washbrook was an extremely popular player with the Old Trafford crowds and his testimonial match against an Australian side led by Don Bradman in 1948 was watched by an estimated 50,000 people. The receipts of £14,000 set a new record not to be broken in money terms until Farokh raised over £26,000 in 1976. By 1968 it was a few years since Washbrook had taken to the field, but Farokh remembers him as a Committee member:

I can't say that he was over friendly, but then there was a big divide between Committee members and players in my day. Only rarely would a Committee member come and speak to a player unless it was after the game. There were exceptions, and Cedric Rhoades and Eric Taylor come immediately to mind, but other Committee members were known to call players by the wrong name and sometimes make hurtful comments behind their backs. I can certainly remember occasions when Cyril Washbrook would come and compliment me for my wicketkeeping or a good innings with the bat but it didn't happen very often – mind you, when it did happen you felt he really meant it. He was a regular watcher of county games but as far as most of the players were concerned he was a bit remote and aloof. That's how it was with the Committee members.

By the time Farokh signed for Lancashire the county had faced an honours drought for some time. The runners-up position in 1960 had been followed

Another day at the office.

by seven consecutive years when Lancashire failed to make the top ten in the championship. In 1962 and 1963 they had been placed sixteenth and fifteenth respectively, their worst ever positions. From that point there was a marginal improvement as the county gradually improved its position by one place each year until reaching eleventh place in 1967. The advent of one-day cricket with the Gillette Cup, which began in 1963, provided some cause for optimism, with Lancashire reaching the semi-finals on three occasions and the quarter-finals once. But still they had not won anything and this was a completely unsatisfactory position for a county with such a distinguished past and some excellent current players. It was clearly part of Farokh's brief to help bring about a turnaround in fortunes.

Much would depend on Lancashire's new captain, Jack Bond. Bond, who began his working life as a clerk for the Electricity Board, had made his Lancashire debut in 1955 when he was dismissed for 0 and 1 by Lock and Laker in a match against Surrey. He had to wait until 1961 before being awarded his county cap after scoring 3 centuries – the first of 14 for his county. The following summer was the best of his career as he scored 2,125 runs including a career best of 157 against Hampshire at Old Trafford. Then,

Photo-finish.

in 1963, he broke his left arm when trying to play a short ball from Wes Hall in a match against the West Indies. As he said to the *Manchester Evening News*:

> I was out for three months and when I recovered I got the impression that no one had any confidence in me. Consequently, my form suffered and I found myself in and out of the side over the next four years.
>
> Then in 1968, just as I was beginning to resign myself to leaving, they gave me the captaincy – and a new lease of life.

Bond admitted that Lancashire's results were dismal and Old Trafford resembled a 'ghost town'. Yet Bond's style of leadership was able to spark a revival and the crowds came flooding back. Farokh was in no doubt as to the capabilities of his new leader:

'Bondy' was one of the finest captains I've played under and we had a great rapport: just one look or glance from behind the stumps and he immediately knew what I was thinking and we could make a decision over a field change without so much as a gesture or whisper. We had a great understanding – if only he had been my bridge partner! He might field in a variety of positions: at gully, mid-on, mid-off, but not many words were exchanged unless it was the end of the over. He was a great captain for the way he held the team together rather than by his example with the bat, ball or in the field. Having said that, he made the most fantastic catch to dismiss Asif Iqbal in the Gillette

Cover drive.

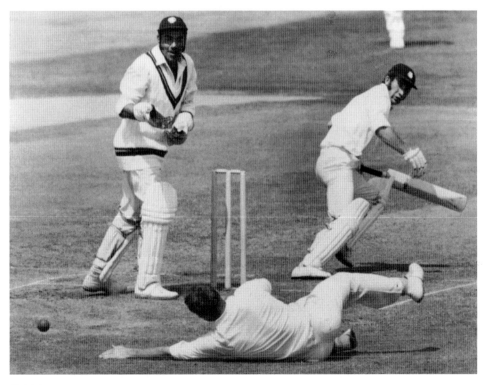

Catch it.

Cup Final at Lord's in 1971 – this catch effectively won us the game. His overall contribution was immense. His man-management was top class and he had it in him to motivate, encourage and inspire. There were no heavy-handed or draconian measures. He treated each player differently, as an individual. He knew we each had our own temperamental styles and he could fathom the psychology of the players. I can honestly say that we never had a single cross word. That isn't to say that there weren't vigorous discussions in the dressing room after a match but the argument was always constructive. Later on, over a glass of beer, we would think of ways we could have performed better – these discussions were usually very fruitful with a number of concrete suggestions coming from other colleagues. 'Bondy' never felt threatened by these discussions because he wanted the same as the rest of us – for the team to win and keep on winning.

When questioned about the secrets of his leadership, Bond revealed some of his methods:

> I like to think I can motivate young players. If they have anything to say to me I don't give them the impression they are talking a lot of rubbish.
>
> My first job on taking over was to restore the players' faith in themselves. Previously they had been accepting defeat before they had even got on to the field.
>
> Not enough attention was being paid to fielding and fitness. By improving our fielding we were able to compensate for any deficiencies in batting and bowling.
>
> At the start of that season, Jack Crompton, Manchester United's trainer, put us through our paces and I remember some of the older players moaning like hell over it.
>
> But after a while everyone realised the importance of peak fitness in this game. After all, the standard of county cricket has evened out just as it has done in soccer. This means that the fittest side is bound to come out on top eventually.
>
> (*Manchester Evening News*, 23 July 1970)

A photograph of the Lancashire side in 1968 shows a team in transition. Of the twelve players pictured, five were shortly to leave Lancashire: Brian Statham, Geoff Pullar, Ken Higgs, John Savage and Graham Atkinson. Both Statham and Pullar were to leave at the end of that season. Nicknamed 'George' and sometimes 'The Whippet', Statham was a right-arm fast bowler and Jack Bond's immediate predecessor as Lancashire captain. Described by Wisden as 'one of the best of all England fast bowlers' he was a regular fixture in the England side for more than a decade, forming partnerships with first Frank Tyson and then Freddie Trueman. He played in 70 Test matches and took 252 Test wickets, a total bettered by only four English bowlers – Botham, Willis,

Trueman and Underwood. John Arlott wrote of Statham: 'He was the most undemonstrative of fast bowlers; a studious technician rather than a flamboyant artist.' His temperament was the very opposite to that of Farokh, yet the two men soon became close friends:

I never played against 'George' in a Test match but we had met in 1967 when India played Lancashire at Southport and I hit a number of his deliveries onto the railway line. Brian actually complimented me on my innings, though I knew in my heart that I had been merely lucky that day and said so as we shared a beer or two after the game. That was the start of my long association with this great man. We used to travel together to most of the away fixtures during my first season with Lancashire and I can remember us stopping off at some of the most obscure and out of the way pubs as we avoided the motorways on our itinerary. It was always a great honour to share his experiences and humility. Travelling from somewhere like Somerset to the North West we would visit at least fifteen watering holes. He loved his beer and his cigarettes and the car was always dense with smoke. All the landlords and publicans knew him. Even if we arrived back in Cheshire at two in the morning he would know of some great little pub where we would gain entrance through the back door after making the right taps on the window.

It always gave me something of a thrill to read 'caught Engineer bowled Statham' or even 'stumped Engineer bowled Statham'. Many fast bowlers would have taken offence at the keeper standing up to the wicket – as a kind of slur on their speed – but not Brian. He even encouraged me to stand close to the wicket for this forced many batsmen to play off their back foot when they should have been on the front. This resulted in a number of additional lbw decisions. Brian once paid me the compliment of telling me that if I had been his wicketkeeper throughout his career he would have doubled his tally of wickets. Whether this was his sincere opinion or not I don't know, but it was so kind and generous for him to say so.

Brian never blew his own trumpet. In fact, I don't think he truly realised how good he was. The man was a genius yet so humble, that's what made him stand out from the rest. When we were in Barbados together he was with his lovely wife, Audrey. I was doing some commentating and I remember once seeing Brian in a crowd of people looking completely lost. I thought, no-one over here even knows that this is the great Brian Statham and when I mentioned it to one or two people their eyebrows were raised: 'This man Statham man?' Brian would rarely tell anyone who he was and this is unusual amongst great cricketers, especially the 'has-beens'. When you have been famous and are suddenly neglected you want to be remembered. I certainly love people to recognise me and I'm sure Freddie Trueman is the

Left: A rare defensive stroke.

Below: Howzat?

Opposite below: Wars of the Roses – part one.

same but not Brian Statham. He was very humble, very unassuming. I wish I had his qualities.

One of Statham's bowling partners who left Lancashire in 1969 was Ken Higgs. In 1968 he was honoured as one of the Wisden Cricketers of the Year, reflecting sterling service to both county and country. As a Test cricketer he played 15 matches celebrating his first appearance for England with 8 wickets against South Africa in 1965. Higgs was the only player to appear in all five Tests against the West Indies in 1966. Given his tally of 71 Test wickets at an average of 20.74, it is perhaps surprising that Higgs did not play for his country more often, but Wisden suggests that this may have been due to a 'dour and undemonstrative' manner and the fact that he was 'unimpressed by figures of authority'. As a Lancashire player Higgs took 7 for 36 in the second innings of his first game for the county against Hampshire at Old Trafford in 1958 and produced a hat-trick against Essex at Blackpool in 1960. His overall county figures were 1033 wickets at an average of 22.9. After leaving Lancashire, Higgs was tempted out of early retirement to play for Leicestershire, who he captained in 1979. As late as 1986, in his fiftieth year, Higgs reappeared for the latter county in an emergency and took 5 for 22 against Yorkshire. Other sporting accomplishments included playing half-back for Port Vale Football Club:

Ken was certainly boisterous, aggressive and bullish – he would order the younger players around. He was always immaculate, very tidy in the dressing room, very domesticated for some reason. And he was petrified of his wife, Mary. He never drove a car, that was with Mary. Mary was his pride and joy, a lovely girl, but she was definitely the boss. I'm sure Ken came up to Old Trafford to work off his aggression on the boys. He would travel by train, which was almost unheard of in those days, and Mary would pick him up at the station. He had little respect for authority, spoke his mind and never mastered the skills of diplomacy – but he was a tremendous cricketer. We got on all right, I think, but he wasn't a great mixer as he always seemed to have a train to catch. Regrettably he left Lancashire rather suddenly after a disagreement with the Committee.

The major gap in Lancashire's batting strength was created by the departure of Geoff Pullar at the end of the 1968 season. The left-hander had joined Lancashire in 1954 and was selected for England as an opening batsman five years later. In his second Test against India in July 1959 he made 131, so becoming the first Lancastrian to score a Test century at Old Trafford – this followed an innings of 137 made against India in a county match at the same ground at the end of June. Pullar, affectionately known as 'Noddy', was on the

Wars of the Roses – part two.

field at Green Park, Kanpur, when Farokh walked to the crease in his first Test match in December 1961. In England's second innings he scored 119. Pullar played in 28 Tests, scoring 1,974 with an average of over 43, but his Test career was brought to a premature close through a knee injury. For Lancashire, Pullar scored 16,583 runs with 32 centuries. His acknowledged qualities were those of determination, concentration and a correct technique, especially in defence; he was also an elegant stroke player. Pullar most endeared himself to Lancashire crowds when, in Yorkshire's championship year of 1959, he scored 3 centuries against the old enemy, including a century before lunch when 'The Rest' played Yorkshire at The Oval. In 1969 he moved to Gloucestershire for two years:

I always thought that Geoff was called 'Noddy' because he used to doze off from time to time but I'm not totally sure – we all had nicknames of one sort or another. I can remember Geoff telling me back in the early 1960s when he was touring India how he could 'pick' Fergie Gupte even sitting in the stands – whether it was going to be a leg-break or a googly or a top-spin. Now Fergie certainly wasn't that easy to 'pick' and I was amazed at the audacity of a foreigner making such a claim. When Pullar came out to bat on one occasion to face the bowling of Gupte I told Fergie to put him to the test and

Another one bites the dust.

he bowled a simple straightforward googly pitched on off stump. Geoff jumped out of the crease to drive it and missed the ball thinking it was a leg-break. I whipped the bails off and Geoff muttered, 'I picked him' as he turned to face the pavilion! But Pullar was a very fine opening bat, a regular guy and a likeable fellow.

Retirements and transfers to other counties meant that Lancashire could refashion their side both through promotion from the ranks and new signings. David Lloyd now became a regular first-team player and Jack Simmons joined the county followed by Frank Hayes and Peter Lee. One of the new recruits who was to have most impact on the fortunes of the club, however, was the West Indian batsman Clive Hubert Lloyd. Lloyd was also to become one of Farokh's closest cricketing associates as well as a great personal friend. Farokh first met Clive Lloyd in early 1967 when the West Indies were touring India and the two cricketers forged a lasting friendship. Lloyd was fielding during Farokh's 109 scored in the Third Test at Madras and this was the first and last time the two men played together until Lloyd followed Farokh as Lancashire's second overseas signing. When Farokh arrived at Lancashire he was asked about the merits of the prospective new signing:

I was consulted before Lancashire appointed Clive. I had seen him play when the West Indies visited India in 1966-67. I thought then that this fellow was a marvellous cricketer with a marvellous eye, and he was a tremendous fielder. His movement on the field was breathtaking, like a cat, a big cat, tall, lanky and relaxed, but when there was a ball near him those muscles certainly moved like a panther. His reflexes were immediate. What an attacking batsman and what an acquisition he would be for Lancashire. I shall never forget that one of the Lancashire committee members, Mr Cyril Washbrook, the great Cyril Washbrook, said, 'Farokh, what do you think of Clive Lloyd?' 'Well you needn't look any further,' I replied, 'You've certainly got the finest that's going. He is, in my opinion, one of the finest and most attractive batsmen in the world today and a brilliant fielder – you sign him on straight away.' 'But Farokh, he wears glasses,' he said. 'Mr Washbrook, forget his glasses, honestly sign him on, get there before anyone else does, don't lose him. We can combine well together and help to make Lancashire a great team.' And, of course, Lancashire signed him on. For away fixtures we were room-mates, we ate, drank and slept together – but insisted on separate beds! We both signed three-year contracts and I think we were at the heart of building up the new spirit of optimism and belief in the team's abilities.

Clive often looked glum and you might think he was very serious-minded but in fact he was a fun-loving guy and we had some great laughs together. We had the same likes and dislikes. We were both party animals and he

Pal, room-mate and partner Clive 'Hubert' Lloyd.

would never say anything about me and vice-versa – a true friend. Some time later I remember flying with Lloydy from Manchester to Sydney and then onto Canberra. We had been invited by the Australian Prime Minister to play for the PM's XI. Bob Hawke was the Prime Minister of Australia. That flight from Manchester to Sydney seemed like a shuttle flight from Manchester to London; we never stopped laughing and before I knew it I was pointing out Sydney Bridge as we came in to land. Incidentally, our wives dread it when we meet because they know we're going to reminisce and wander off together.

It was just as well that Lloyd had a good sense of humour for, as David Lloyd relates, when Clive arrived in Lancashire the club housed him in the centre of Manchester at an address, Unit Two Sauna, which would have instantly revealed its true nature to more worldly eyes. It appears that the club remained oblivious as to where they had sent their new star and Clive found himself sleeping on a 'massage bed'.

This was an unfortunate beginning for someone who turned out to be one of the true cricketing greats. Despite the thick glasses resulting from an eye injury sustained at the age of twelve when the young Clive was attempting to break up a school fight, he went on to become the first West Indian to win 100 Test caps, the captain of the West Indies in 74 Tests, leading his side to two

Seventies man.

World Cup victories at Lord's and eleven successive wins in 1984. In 1976 he scored 201 not out against Glamorgan in just 120 minutes, so becoming the joint record holder for the fastest ever first-class double hundred. Lloyd also captained Lancashire from 1981-83 and in 1986. He scored 12,764 runs for his county at an average of 44.94, including 30 centuries and 71 half-centuries. As a useful right-arm medium-pace bowler he took 55 wickets at an average of 32.89 with his best figures being 4 for 48 against Leicestershire at Old Trafford in 1970.

Jackie Bond was fortunate in that he soon inherited all the ingredients necessary to convert an 'also-ran' side into one that could win trophies. After the departure of Statham, Pullar and John Savage, who remained with the club as a coach, there was a preponderance of younger players. Their enthusiasm, energy and determination to succeed were an important part of the formula that was to restore pride and confidence to the club. Youth also implied minds that were ready to learn, athleticism on the field and good levels of physical fitness. There was now an excellent blend of overseas talent, budding England players (Barry Wood, Peter Lever, David Lloyd and Ken Shuttleworth) and dependable county stalwarts (Harry Pilling, David Hughes, John Sullivan and Jack Simmons). Provided this potential could be realised, there was no reason why Lancashire should not return to the top flight of cricketing counties. What was in many ways so surprising was the speed with which this transformation was achieved. But then with players of the temperament of Farokh Engineer and Clive Lloyd in the side, one could not expect a slow, patient build-up to glory. Both Lancashire and all the players wanted a dramatic and, if possible, immediate change in fortunes.

nine

Lancashire, La La La

Farokh spent nine happy seasons with Lancashire, during which time the club was able to celebrate something almost every year – either an improvement in championship form as happened in 1968, when Lancashire went from eleventh to sixth position, or a trophy or a place in the final for one of the one-day competitions. The only entirely lean year was 1973, when a championship position of twelfth was accompanied by fourth position in the John Player League, a quarter-final place in the Gillette Cup and a semi-final place in the Benson & Hedges Cup. In every other year there was some kind of honour: John Player League Champions in 1969 and 1970, Gillette Cup winners in 1970, 1971, 1972 and 1975 and Gillette Cup losing finalists in 1974 and 1976. This was a remarkable run of success by any standards and owed everything to a comparatively recent cricketing innovation – the introduction of one-day cricket.

In fact, a cricketing cup competition had been tried in the nineteenth century following an MCC resolution of 1873, but the experiment had ended in failure when four of the original six contenders withdrew from the competition after the first round. The idea of limited-over, one-day cricket was conceived by another MCC committee established in 1956. The driving force behind the discussions was the dramatic decline in attendances and therefore the finances of many first-class counties. In the immediate post-war years more than 2 million paying customers would pass the turnstiles to watch first-class County Championship cricket. Owing to a variety of factors, including the expansion of alternative leisure opportunities and improvements in communications, attendances declined during the 1950s so that by 1963 turnstile numbers were below 720,000. It was hoped that the introduction of a one-day knock-out competition would help to restore popular interest in the game. The Gillette Cup began in 1963 with all the seventeen first-class counties taking part. By 1964 the competition was extended to include the previous season's top Minor Counties and the original over allocation was

Lancashire's winning formula – the dynamic dozen.

'Bond'ing with silverware.

Over the bowler's head.

reduced from 65 to 60. The John Player League, to be played on Sunday afternoons and early evenings, was introduced in 1969. Overs were set at 40 for each side and bowlers were restricted to a 15-yard run-up. Finally, the Benson & Hedges Competition was introduced in 1972. Its structure resembled that of the Ranji Trophy in that regional leagues led onto a knock-out competition. Farokh was all in favour of the new developments:

I enjoyed one-day cricket immensely. One-day cricket filled a big gap, a big vacuum. We needed the football-type supporters, we needed a game that had a result at the end of the day. We didn't want to play for five days and fail to get a result. That could be disheartening, although from a technical point of view there could be just as much skill in grafting and working to save a game as in scoring winning runs. There was obviously great skill in Test cricket. It was like a game of chess, it was a mind game; but one-day cricket could be tremendous. It has improved batting, improved bowling and particularly fielding. Players know that they have a target of getting so many runs per over and batsmen are always looking for shots, always taking risks because of the absence of so many slip fielders. In Test cricket you can afford to take your time and play safe; this is much less the case in the one-day game.

One-day cricket ideally suited my temperament. I was just born to be a one-day player; for my type of cricket it was ideal. Unfortunately there wasn't much of it about in my time apart from the success we had in the Gillette Cup and John Player League, which I thoroughly enjoyed. One-day cricket should never replace the traditional longer game but it should exist alongside the three, four or five-day match. Certainly one-day cricket is here to stay, make no mistake, for it is obviously so much more popular than the five-day Test, but there are different skills required and I think the two games should be played in harness with one another.

In terms of wicketkeeping I was definitely more aggressive during the one-day game, although I was usually aggressive, even in a Test match. By 'aggressive' I mean standing close up to the stumps. In a Test match this isn't so necessary because there will be several slips and the batsman doesn't often go out of his crease. In the one-day game, in order to score quicker runs the batsmen are constantly leaving the crease in order to drive the ball, so providing every opportunity for a stumping. Standing close to the stumps also keeps the batsman on the back foot, restricting his shots, encouraging lbw decisions and cramping his style. It unsettles the batsman when the keeper is only inches away. His body space is invaded and he can't relax – all part of the psychological warfare. But to do this you have to be quick, especially if the ball is going down the leg side from the pace bowlers. In order to stand right up to the wicket you have to have the confidence that you have the speed to make the right movements. I had that confidence.

The Lancashire revival and Farokh's new career got off to a faltering start with the county losing to Nottinghamshire in the first round of the Gillette Cup and then losing to Kent, Worcestershire and Yorkshire before registering their first County Championship match victory against Middlesex in mid-June 1968. Farokh scored his first fifty for his new club against Worcestershire in a drawn game beginning on 18 May, but was not able to repeat the feat until the end of June in a game against Warwickshire. *The Manchester Evening News* reported the innings with the headline 'Engineer in form – slams 54':

> Farokh Engineer launched a furious assault on West Indian Test spinner Lance Gibbs here today… The Indian hit a six and four boundaries in his display of aggression combined with caution… After reaching his half-century out of 68 in 90 minutes, Engineer was bowled by Cartwright with one that came back after pitching. Engineer had done a great job…
>
> (*Manchester Evening News*, 29 June 1968)

In the following match Farokh made 70, batting at number 2, against Somerset – one reporter commented that Engineer looked 'on every ball with distaste as something to be batted out of sight'. This was to be his highest score during

I'll take that Lloydy.

the 1968 season. The journalist James Mossop enthused over this innings and wrote his report under the headline, 'Majestic Lancashire get a taste of that old glory':

> You would have to plough through the memoirs of the Old Trafford longroom – a place where venerable members watch the cricket on high stools – to find anything like yesterday's events. For, on a summer day of golden vintage, Lancashire stalked the arena with an unreal majesty... It gave Lancashire's committee a chance to push aside the brickbats and smile benignly on their most recent recruit, Farokh Engineer. At last, sighed the crowd at the end of a morning and afternoon of boredom, here is a batsman of imagination. Engineer, as industrious as his name, was also daring, courageous and colourful. He thumped the first ball of the innings for four and never let up.... His 70 included seven fours and a six, scored in 115 enthralling minutes.

But with only 3 half-centuries made during the season Farokh was obviously having some teething problems with the bat, though there was nothing but praise for his wicketkeeping – a *Manchester Evening News* headline of 6 June read 'Brilliant Engineer Takes Flying Catch'.

John Kay commented after Lancashire's first win of the season:

Way over the top – Mike Procter's bouncer.

Farokh Engineer has yet to strike form. It's fair to say that Farokh has not had one lucky break so far this summer. He has played on several times, been the victim of superb catches, and has also been snapped up off the bat and pad when not quite getting the ball in the middle of the bat.

Things would soon improve during the 1969 season. Meanwhile, Farokh had had his first encounter with a cricketing legend, the Yorkshire and England fast bowler, Freddie Trueman:

I was driving with Brian Statham to Headingley and on the way 'George' jokingly asked me if I had met Fred before. I replied that I hadn't but that I was very much looking forward to meeting such a great fast bowler, one of the greatest English fast bowlers of all time. I had read and heard so much about him. When we arrived at Headingley we went directly to the visitors' dressing room with the Yorkshire dressing room right next to ours. And who walks in stark naked but for a pipe and a jockstrap but the great Fred Trueman. 'Hello George, sunshine,' he said. I was changing next to Statham who introduced me. 'Mr Trueman,' I said, (we were always taught to respect our elders and senior cricketers) 'I have heard so much about you and it's a real pleasure meeting you, sir.' And his very first words to me were 'Don't you f—ing creep to me, lad'. He then addressed Statham: 'George, this guy has hit one of the fastest and most spectacular Test hundreds... when he comes out to bat, have a look to see if I'm bowling because if the phone goes for him, you can tell the caller to hang on... he'll soon be back to the f—ing pavilion... nice meeting you, son.' I just smiled but Fred's prediction came true, more or less, and he claimed my wicket when I was on 13 – but not before I'd hooked him for a flat six with a ball that thumped against the Headingley pavilion at mid-wicket and rebounded half way across the pitch. This was followed by another hook for four followed by a near boundary when we ran for 3.

Fred Trueman also remembers this encounter and describes the delivery which eventually claimed Farokh's wicket:

> I've only bowled once at Farokh Engineer and that was during the twilight of my career... I'd heard a lot about his approach to the game and I was prepared for a real battle. I knew he was partial to the hook and so I decided to apply the Trueman logic – a nasty rising short ball with just enough about it to tempt the hook. And Farokh, never one for missing an opportunity, did just that. But he didn't really connect. In fact, the ball hit him on the wrist and trickled down onto the wicket.

Trueman's bowling figures for the Lancashire first innings in the twilight of his career were 5 for 45. It may have been this achievement that led to some uncharacteristic behaviour that evening:

After the day's play we were in the Committee room having a drink – none of the players had to pay for their drinks – and Fred asked me what I'd like to have. I requested a glass of beer and he went up to the bar and got me a drink. The Yorkshire players swear that they had never seen Fred fetch a drink before for a member of the opposition. I took this as a considerable compliment.

After the relatively modest achievements for both player and county of the 1968 season things suddenly took off. The glory trail began with a Sunday match against Sussex at Hove in late April, which Lancashire won by 5 wickets with 12 balls to spare. Clive Lloyd was now playing for the county and the two foreign players scored more than half the Lancashire total. E.W. Swanton wrote of how Farokh had 'sparkled behind the stumps (especially on the leg-side)' and continued to do so with the bat with his innings of 31. Continuing to play at number 2, Farokh impressed again in the match against Nottinghamshire

Has he snicked it?

on 11 May when he scored 46 of Lancashire's 179 runs. This was the first Sunday League fixture to be played at Old Trafford and the home side won by 47 runs in front of a disappointingly small crowd of under 1,000. According to a cricketing correspondent, 'Engineer, who hit five excellent boundaries, was Lancashire's best batsman' and scored his runs in an hour 'to set a scoring pace that was always ahead of the clock'. Another useful innings followed against Somerset on 6 July. According to Alan Dunn, 'Engineer was delightful, smashing powerful fours with great abandon all round the wicket and hooking a huge six.' In the Somerset innings Farokh had dived sharply left to claim the wicket of Greg Chappell with a 'superb catch'.

Undoubtedly Farokh's most memorable Sunday League performance, however, came in the very next week when Lancashire played Glamorgan at Southport on 13 July. It was in the course of this innings that the Glamorgan former captain and fast bowler, Ossie Wheatley, was heard to remark, 'I do not mind him charging, but I do wish he would let me set off first'. Farokh's 78 not out won universal admiration:

Farokh Engineer, bat flashing like a scimitar, tore Glamorgan apart yesterday as Lancashire, supreme exponents of single-day cricket, raced to their eighth successive victory. The Indian wicketkeeper scorned the stealthy approach which would have enabled his side just as surely to pass the 112 Glamorgan had scratched together. And in just 76 minutes, he drove, hooked, and at times snicked his way to an unbeaten 78 which gave Lancashire a nine wickets success. His carefree, but seldom careless pursuit of runs thrilled a crowd of more than 10,000 at Southport where the gates were locked with hundreds still queueing outside. Glamorgan were helpless before the onslaught. Their field spread fearfully to the boundary edge like some huge umbrella, whenever he took strike. But still it was pierced by ten cruel blows for four, and one six swung mightily to mid-wicket off Nash…He finally fell to a catch behind the wicket with Lancashire a mere five runs from home.

Ted Corbett of the *Daily Mirror* described the innings as 'magnificent', while Peter Smith wrote that Engineer played 'as if he were rushing for an early train' delivering 'a mixture of crisp straight drives, saucy cuts and full-blooded pulls'. Under the headline 'Glamorgan Butchered', Eric Todd of *The Guardian* delivered an admiring assessment:

Engineer quite rightly was yesterday's popular hero and when he is in this mood there is no more attractive nor destructive batsman in the business. Sometimes, of course, he appears to take leave of his senses and gets himself out to strokes that would send any conscientious coach into premature retirement. At other times he is visited by inspiration or genius and then his batting has the blessings of the angels and archangels. This was an occasion for the latter. Engineer cut and drove imperiously and impudently. He pranced down the wicket and drove Wheatley for two fours and two twos in his second over. He advanced and thrashed Cordle and Nash. And when a 'wag' in the crowd yelled: 'Step on it Lancs,' Engineer pulled Nash for six. Engineer also hit 10 fours and never gave a chance, never gave Glamorgan a hope… Not often this season will a holiday crowd be given better entertainment. And not often will a holiday crowd be so enthusiastic.

Farokh and Clive Lloyd were obviously a major part in Lancashire's one-day success. But as Farokh would be the first to admit, what made Lancashire so special during those glory years was the overall team contribution. Jack Bond even banned the display of averages on the dressing room wall until the end of the season. David Lloyd, Jack Simmons and David Hughes, all future Lancashire captains, were important figures in the Lancashire revival. Described by Christopher Martin-Jenkins as a 'chirpy, intelligent Accrington lad', David Lloyd, affectionately known as 'Bumble' on account of his 'engaging Lancashire burr', arrived at Lancashire CCC in 1965:

Warming up.

Bumble always spoke a great game of cricket, he could conjure up a great tale from nothing. No wonder he is in such demand as an after-dinner speaker; he is also an excellent commentator. We would sometimes open the Lancashire innings together and he was a great man to have in the dressing room because he could make everyone laugh. Definitely one of the funniest men around. I remember when he made his 214 not out against India at Edgbaston in 1974. I wished him luck as he came to the crease because I wanted to see him score some runs – but not that many! He was a great thinker about the game.

Jack Simmons had joined Lancashire in the same year as Farokh, though he had previously been involved with the club as a junior before playing Lancashire League cricket:

Jack was a great pro, a typical league man. He was also at the centre of the team, one of the nicest persons I've come across, a lovely warm man who

Warmed up.

was totally genuine and gave his heart out 100 per cent to Lancashire – it's only right that he was awarded the MBE and is now the Chairman of Lancashire. He thinks Lancastrian, he drinks Lancastrian... he's Lancastrian through and through. I can't see a bigger Lancashire man than Jack Simmons. He was also a character; Jack was larger than life. At times he acted as our team manager, representing players in their dealings with the Committee. Although we called him 'Flatjack' his bowling was extremely effective – even the great Barry Richards had difficulty scoring off him, especially in one-day games. 'Simmo' was not a Test match bowler but he did wonders. With the bat he could often make a quick score. At one point Jack went out to Tasmania to do some coaching and did a fantastic job by all accounts. He helped to launch the cricketing career of David Boon – he was so grateful that he named his son after Jack.

David Hughes, who also played for Tasmania, joined Lancashire the year before Farokh and remained with the club for more than twenty years:

Unorthodox but effective.

David 'Yoza' Hughes was a very good cricketer, a brilliant fielder and a very keen student of the game. He made his name in a semi-final of the Gillette Cup played at Old Trafford in July 1971. It was getting late and the light was fading when David came out to bat approaching nine o'clock. Gloucestershire very sportingly put the off-spinner John Mortimer on to bowl – they could have used Mike Procter – and David hit 24 runs in an over to win the match. David was a friendly, humorous character and this was typical of the whole side. Everyone was so friendly with each other, it was like a big family with everyone rooting for each other and wanting everyone to do well. Jack Bond united the side beautifully – despite the prima donnas everyone blended into the team.

Lancashire's pace bowling attack consisted of two England players, Peter Lever and Ken Shuttleworth, together with Peter Lee:

We nicknamed Peter Lever 'Plank'. He was pretty brisk, well in the 80mph region if not faster, in fact, he once nearly killed a New Zealand player with one of his deliveries. Peter and I had a little rapport in that although he had a perfectly legitimate action, he could 'ping' or throw the odd one. When this happened I could feel the ball thud in my gloves straight away because it was not far short of the 90mph delivery. I used to look at him and he would give me a wink. Every bowler chucks the odd one and Peter Lever was no exception, but he admitted to it whereas a lot of bowlers don't. Throwing is definitely an art and great bowlers use the technique in a deceptive manner.

Ken Shuttleworth was known as 'Rasputin' because he could lose his rag very quickly if a decision went against him or he was no-balled a few times – he would snatch his sweater from the umpire. He was a fiery character but a great bowler with a brilliant action and he should surely have played for England more often than he did. He also had a very dry sense of humour and seemed to know virtually every country lane short-cut in the land.

Peter Lee, 'Leapy Lee', was our third seamer, signed from Northants. He bowled an exceedingly good line and length, he was quick and could cut the ball off the seam in both directions. He was extremely effective and used to take 100 wickets a season for Lancashire. He was tremendous but very underrated; I've hardly heard anyone mention Peter Lee – one hell of a good bowler. It was great fun keeping wicket to these three after equally rewarding experiences keeping to the great Brian Statham and Ken Higgs.

In mid-August 1969 Farokh broke a finger in a drawn county match against Sussex at Hove. The Lancashire captain later explained to the press just how much the club were missing their recent acquisition:

> Lancashire did not suffer just one blow… We suffered two – because it needed two players to replace him, a wicket keeper and an opening bat. This was a great loss for us for Engineer has had a first-rate season. He has had a hard season too, scoring nearly 1,000 runs in championship cricket, over 300 in Sunday League games, and keeping wicket immaculately. It is not often you get a wicket keeper capable of opening the innings – and to be honest it isn't fair to ask a man to do it. No other wicket keeper in the world to my knowledge does it. It was more common in the past, but it is asking a lot when you are playing seven days a week… I know he is itching to be back in the side. Engineer is one of those cricketers who thoroughly enjoys the Sunday game. It's just another ball game to me – a game different from championship cricket, whereas for Engineer it's sheer enjoyment, a game to delight in.
>
> (*Manchester Evening News*, August 1969)

Following the title success in the inaugural season of the Sunday League, Farokh continued to shine in the competition and the summer of 1970 provided the occasion for a host of sparkling innings. Two of these stand out:

his 49 out of a total of 94 scored against Middlesex in April and his 46 scored against Derbyshire at Buxton on 19 July. The match against Middlesex at Old Trafford was the first Player League game of the season. The *Daily Mail* referred to Farokh's 'dazzling 49 off 46 deliveries' under the headline 'Engineer Inspires Champions' Easy Win'. John Arlott described a 'commanding innings' and called Farokh's batting 'an exhilarating start to any season'. Middlesex had scored 93, setting Lancashire a striking rate of almost 3.5 an over in showery conditions. According to Arlott:

> Engineer was in his most exuberant mood, and he took 15 runs from five balls off Connolly's second over... Engineer swept ahead. He cut and drove outstandingly, and stepped inside anything near the leg stump and struck it hard and sometimes high to leg. At times, too, he edged with impunity through the unmanned slip region.

Peter West wrote how Engineer 'lit this baleful spring yesterday with an innings of such authority, charm and impudence that it might have been high summer'. John Kay's opinion was that Farokh's innings consisted of 'discriminate hitting, not just wild slogging' with most of the boundary shots in front of the wicket. He added in a separate article that:

> It was certainly Engineer at his best. It has taken him two seasons to realise the necessity for a patient approach to the game on English pitches, but from now on I reckon Farokh is going to take heavy toll with the bat.

In the match against Derbyshire, Lancashire batted first. There were 8,000 spectators who 'treated the occasion like a football Cup-tie, with raucous cheers and counter cheers, and ballads reminiscent of Wembley or the Stretford End'. A 'hurricane opening partnership' by Engineer and Snellgrove put on 77 in 9 overs. Farokh has clear but frustrating memories of the occasion:

I was a serious contender for winning a substantial money prize for the fastest televised fifty of the competition. My score of 46 had been made from only 26 deliveries and I was really blasting the Derbyshire bowling attack. I hit one ball to deep square leg towards the direction of Fred Rumsey who probably wasn't the quickest of fielders but the ball was travelling speedily towards him. I called for an easy single with my eyes on Rumsey rather than my batting partner, Ken Snellgrove. When I was almost at the non-striker's end I realised that Snellgrove was still in his crease and at a late stage he shouted 'No!' I had to return to my end and was run out. The team was furious with Snellgrove because the prize money would have been divided amongst the players, but we soon forgave him. He was a fine opening player and an extremely skilful three-card brag player as Ces Pepper once discovered to his chagrin when he had three kings to Snellgrove's three aces – this led to the only occasion I can recollect of a game being delayed by a game of cards; when we went out to bat I warned 'Snelly' not to let the ball so much as touch his pads as Pepper had just lost his week's umpiring wages.

The John Player League championship title was accompanied in 1970 by the first of four Gillette Cup trophies to be won by Lancashire during Farokh's nine-year tenure with the club. In this competition Farokh tended to bat lower down in the order than for the Sunday League games, resulting in a number of not out scores – he was 31 not out in his first final against Sussex at Lord's in September 1970. With the Gillette Cup being a knock-out competition it was possible to win the trophy with as few as four games, as happened in 1970, 1972 and 1975. In total, Farokh played in 29 Gillette Cup matches, 24 of which resulted in wins for Lancashire. During the course of this progress he took 40 catches, made 6 stumpings and scored 424 runs. For the Sunday League he played in 102 matches, took 95 catches, made 21 stumpings and scored 2,143 runs. With so much success in the one-day variety of the game it is perhaps surprising that Lancashire were unable to repeat their success with the Benson & Hedges Cup introduced in 1972. Farokh remained uninspired by the new competition:

For some reason the Benson & Hedges Cup was a bit of a jinx for Lancashire. For some reason it didn't appeal to us. We regarded the Gillette Cup as ours. When we played in this competition we believed in ourselves but after the Lord Mayor's show comes this Benson & Hedges Cup. There was probably a bit too much one-day cricket around at this point and we never really took to it, it never grabbed our imagination. Nor did it bring out the best in our players. It may have been a case of one-day cricket fatigue – there are only so many furrows you can plough and this was the newcomer. It could never compete with the Gillette Cup, which was regarded as the FA Cup of the cricket world. We never took to the Benson & Hedges Cup and it never really took to us.

Similarly, Lancashire were unable to reproduce their one-day form in the County Championship. The improvement to 6th position in 1968 was immediately followed by a drop to 15th, though 3rd position was attained in 1970 and 1971. After that Lancashire's rating was inconsistent: 15th, 12th, 8th, 4th and 16th. Farokh explains this relatively poor performance as partly related to the reputation Lancashire had acquired in the one-day game:

We had some very attacking batsmen in our side who were capable of making a mockery of reasonable declarations – this happened on a number of occasions. Once or twice Clive Lloyd and I made the runs with half an hour to spare yet it had originally seemed an impossible declaration. And we got the runs so quickly that word soon spread around the county grounds that only the most cautious of declarations would be safe when the opponents were Lancashire. It wasn't just Clive and myself. There was John Sullivan who was one of the finest strikers of the ball – if someone had to get 15 runs in 3 balls, he was your man, such a sweet timer of the ball. There was also Harry Pilling, a great little player, a real gritty batsman who, in my opinion should have played for England – I think he was disadvantaged by being from the north of England, I'm sure he would have been selected if he had been playing for one of the southern counties. And then there was Frank Hayes, who had more potential than any younger player I had seen at that point, and Barry Wood, a serious batsman in the Boycott mould. We had some tremendous batting strength and other sides were forced to treat us with respect. Unfortunately that meant taking few chances, which meant draws rather than results.

The second reason was the weather. We certainly had a fair amount of rain so the pitches weren't so good for batting, the outfields were sluggish and balls slippery. It was so frustrating for us sitting in the dressing room and hearing scores from down south where the sun was shining and where matches could be finished and won. We lost a lot of points that way. Of course there were also some occasions when members of the Lancashire team would be away playing for their country, which reduced the strength of the club side.

In total Farokh played 175 first-class matches for his county, scoring 5,942 runs, making 429 catches and 35 stumpings. Only three Lancashire wicketkeepers – George Duckworth, Warren Hegg and Richard Pilling – have taken more wickets for their county but they also played in more matches. In 1970 Farokh topped the tables for the most dismissals in a season with 82 for his county and 91 in all first-class games. He dismissed six batsmen in an innings against Northamptonshire at Liverpool in 1970 and against Surrey at The Oval in the same year. He dismissed eight batsmen in a match four times: against Somerset at Taunton in 1969, against Northamptonshire at Liverpool in 1970, against Middlesex at Lord's in 1970, and against Nottinghamshire at old Trafford in 1973. In each case all the dismissals were caught. With the bat Farokh's highest score for Lancashire was 141 made against Derbyshire at Buxton in 1971. He scored 3 other centuries: 103 not out against Glamorgan at Swansea in 1969, 128 not out against Surrey at The Oval in 1973 and 104 not out against Warwickshire at Old Trafford in 1975.

Alan Clemison called Farokh's 141 against Derbyshire 'a magnificently disciplined innings'. Derbyshire had declared at 300 for 6 in their first innings. In reply Lancashire were soon 33 for 4 having lost the wickets of David Lloyd for 8, Wood for 10, Pilling for a duck and Clive Lloyd for 7. Batting at number 6, Farokh walked out to the crease to join Ken Snellgrove. In the early part of

A favourite victim – Geoff Boycott.

his innings he 'was circumspect enough for any Test batsman, gaining most of his runs with placed off-side shots and perfectly timed pulls off his toes'. By tea he had reached 96 in a rather untypically steady and responsible innings. Things were about to change:

> A more typical Engineer appeared afterwards. He hooked Ward's second ball savagely to square leg for four and repeated the treatment with his next two deliveries. In the next over, with the crowd cheering wildly, he again hit Ward for three fours. He favoured Buxton with two delicate leg glances to the boundary. When at last he was bowled by Russell the light went out of the day.

One of Farokh's missed opportunities, illustrating both his strengths and weaknesses, came in a game against Yorkshire, as related by Eric Todd of *The Guardian*:

> The Roses' match in August 1969 at Bramhall Lane was among the most exciting of them all. Yorkshire, needing 65 to win, made only 64 of them but because they had four wickets left, the result was a draw and not a tie. It was a narrow escape for Lancashire who were put out in their second innings for 183 towards which Farokh Engineer and Clive Lloyd contributed 140 for the third wicket.
>
> Engineer's own share was 96, and few other batsmen would have attempted to complete a century with a six. A four, four singles, a three and a single, or a brace of twos were far too commonplace to warrant consideration. It just had to be a six and a massive one at that. So Engineer lashed out at

Cope and fell to a simple catch by Hutton at mid on. He departed muttering to himself something like 'Rooky, you silly man. What makes you do these daft things?'

Despite indifferent rankings in the County Championship, Farokh remembers his years with Lancashire as a golden era:

Lancashire played very attractive and exciting cricket and the club membership mushroomed. People would come from miles to see us play. From the Old Trafford dressing room we could see the Warwick Road railway station and as the time for the game approached we would see packed trains emptying the passengers onto the platform ready to make their way to the ground. We could hear the chanting, 'Lancashire, La, La, La' and the excited chatter and laughter. Our popularity was immense, with all the team players receiving regular fan mail – our lockers would be stuffed full of requests for autographs and invitations to parties and other functions. Everyone was talking about us, everyone was buzzing, all over the country, and this buzz lasted for all my years with the club. We were on a roll; we were the Manchester United of cricket.

But just as vivid as the memories of success were the moments of human comedy which rarely enter the record books or newspaper reports. Farokh remembers when Peter Lever was bowling to the Derbyshire batsman Ashley Harvey Walker:

We were playing at Buxton on a very bad pitch, such that the ball was bouncing in a wild, unpredictable way. Lever's first ball missed Harvey Walker's face by a whisker. Worried about facial damage, he then removed his false teeth and gave them to the square leg umpire wrapped in a handkerchief.

Another instance concerns the diminutive practical joker, Harry Pilling. Aware of Farokh's obsession with personal cleanliness, he deposited his grimy jockstrap in Farokh's kitbag on top of the freshly washed and ironed clothes. On arriving at the away fixture dressing room, Farokh and Clive Lloyd decided to teach their teammate a lesson by burning the offending article. But it was so unsavoury that even the flames took nearly half an hour to destroy it.

Harry Pilling was a mere 5ft 2in yet one of his closest cricketing colleagues was Norman Graham who played for Kent. Graham was a giant – Farokh describes him as 'the tallest man I've ever seen' – and it provided 'a great sight to see the two men side by side in the local pub'.

Apart from the moments of comedy it was the camaraderie and the team spirit that made Lancashire such a wonderful club for Farokh. After three years his contract was renewed and then again after a further three years. It was

Retire hurt? No way!

A hero's welcome after a match-winning stumping.

OFFICIAL SOUVENIR BROCHURE

1976 benefit
brochure cover.

important not to break up a winning side. But when finally the heart of Jack Bond's team began to disintegrate the honours became as elusive as before the glory years. After Farokh left Lancashire at the end of the 1976 season it was another eight years before the next trophy, this time the Benson & Hedges Cup, was secured. There seems to have been a magical combination of players during the late sixties and early to mid-seventies, a combination that excited spectators and brought success to the club. Farokh was undoubtedly a key man in this explosion of talent, energy and entertainment.

ten

India's Number One

During his eight seasons with Lancashire, Farokh continued to play Test cricket for India. He was selected for every series between 1968 and 1975 with the exception of the tour to the West Indies in 1970-71. In fact, when he joined Lancashire, Farokh's Test career was exactly at the halfway stage, since he played 23 Tests during these years excluding his matches for the Rest of the World against England and Pakistan in 1970 and Australia in 1971-72. Of the six series in which Farokh played during the second half of his Test career three were against England with one series each against New Zealand, Australia and the West Indies. The highlights included a major contribution to India's win at The Oval in August 1971, so securing India's first series win against England in England, and a century scored against England at the Brabourne Stadium on 6 February 1973. Undoubtedly Farokh's most disappointing moment was when he was out for a pair in his final Test match against the West Indies in January 1975.

Farokh's personal experiences with the bat during these series reflected the general state of India's cricket. When he was performing below par, the national team disappointed, but as Farokh's runs began to flow so did India's fortunes rise. Expectations were high for the three Test series against New Zealand in 1969-70. After all, in the previous series against New Zealand India had achieved their first series win on foreign soil and the opponents were regarded as lambs for the slaughter when they visited India. Things started well and in the First Test played at the Brabourne Stadium, India won by 60 runs with Farokh contributing 20 and 9, but from that point, perhaps through overconfidence, the Indian players seemed to lose their heads. New Zealand won the Second Test at Nagpur by 167 runs having won the toss and scored 319 in the first innings. Batting at number 9 Farokh made creditable contributions of 40 and 19 which together constituted the second highest aggregate Indian score of the match – Abid Ali made the highest with a total of 63. Owing to injury Farokh then missed the final Hyderabad Test and was

Through the covers in Australia.

replaced by Indrajitsinhji. This was almost certainly a good match to miss, for although the result was a draw, India should have been beaten having been bowled out for 89 in their first innings and ending up at 76 for 7 in their second. The match was enveloped in bad odour; the umpires forgot to order the cutting of the pitch on the rest day, so facilitating the penetration of the New Zealand pace attack; the military were used to quell unruly crowd behaviour; the players were accused of living things up and the captain, Pataudi, finally left the field to a chorus of boos. The series was drawn but every Indian cricketer felt that his country had underperformed.

No one expected the Australians to be anything other than the toughest of opposition when their tour of India began in late October 1969. They had retained the Ashes against England in 1968 and then beaten the West Indies at home. There was still disappointment, however, at the 3-1 defeat, especially since the Indian spin attack had effectively contained the Australian batting – 348 was the highest Australian total on the tour. The root cause of the Indian defeat seemed to lie in a number of batting collapses which, in turn, was seen to reflect a lack of determination or will to win. Responsibility was laid at the feet of the captain Pataudi, who was replaced by Wadekar at the end of the series. The Indian psyche may also have been disturbed by riots in Bombay and Calcutta which, in the latter case, had resulted in six fatalities and nearly

100 injured. The immediate causes of these disturbances were dismay at the team performance triggered by, in the case of Bombay, a questionable umpiring decision and, in the case of Calcutta, a shortage of seats allied to suspicions of ticket corruption. It was perhaps unfortunate for Farokh that his best performances were at the beginning of the tour, for the Indian selectors were bound to be influenced by the results of the final 2 Tests in which he failed to score more than 10 runs in 3 of his 4 innings. Furthermore, there was one point in the final Test at Madras when Australia were at 82 for 4 and Walters, on 4, was beaten by Bedi and stranded down the wicket but Farokh uncharacteristically missed the stumping. Walters went on to make 102 and Australia won the match by 77 runs. Farokh's best contribution had been in the second drawn Test at Kanpur when, opening the batting, he scored 77 and 21 – an aggregate score only bettered by Mankad and Viswanath. He also helped India to their only win in the series at Delhi by stumping both Stackpole and Taber in the Australian first innings and then making India's second highest score of 38 in India's reply. All this counted for little, however, when Vijay Merchant, the recently appointed Chairman of the Selectors, decided to adopt a new broom approach in readiness for the tour of the West Indies of 1970-71.

It still rankles with Farokh that he was omitted from the victorious touring side of the West Indies which began in February 1971:

I went home especially to make myself available but the Chairman of the Selectors said to me, 'What can we select you on – the newspaper reports?' Certainly one or two of the Indian selectors took a dim view of the fact that I was playing county cricket in England – something that much improved my game – and I was virtually asked to withdraw from the team for reasons that still baffle me. It was politically motivated; it was beautifully engineered by the so-called powers that be. I was in my prime and I think I could have contributed a lot to the series. My replacement, Pochiah Krishnamurthy, was playing for the South Zone and the politics came from that area – they wanted their own man in and Farokh Engineer was sacrificed. I just couldn't believe the things that were going on in Indian cricket. They frustrated me and drove me out of the country. I just couldn't stomach the pettiness, the divisiveness and the manoeuvrings of certain officials who knew little about the game but had their own agendas. They have done immeasurable harm to Indian cricket and quite simply decided that they didn't want me to tour with the Indian team.

If one wanted to find reasons for Farokh's exclusion it could be argued that it was time for him to make way for a younger player, or that his performances with the bat against New Zealand and Australia had lacked consistency, but the arguments for his inclusion were far weightier. In the summer of 1970 a scheduled South African tour of England had been cancelled on account of

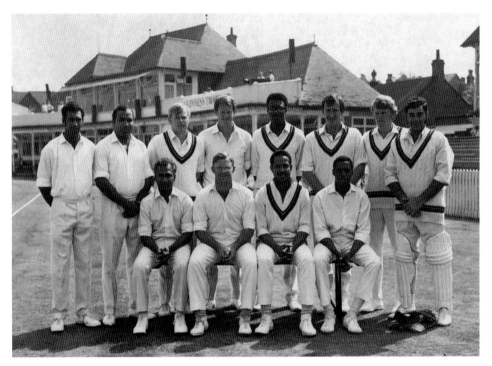

The only Indian player in the World XI, 1970.

Keeping for the World XI, 1970.

Above left: D'Oliveira caught behind off Sobers, June 1970. *Above right:* Edrich caught Engineer, England *v.* World XI, July 1970.

the apartheid issue. In place of this tour a Rest of the World XI was chosen to play 5 Tests against England and Farokh was selected as the wicketkeeper for the first 2 Tests played at Lord's and Trent Bridge. He was the only Indian player selected for this side, which included such legends as Barry Richards, Mike Procter and the captain, Gary Sobers. At the Lord's Test played in June Farokh took 6 catches and made 1 stumping. In December 1970 Farokh again played for a Rest of the World side against Pakistan in Karachi. There was absolutely no doubt that Farokh was the best Indian wicketkeeper and there were many who acclaimed him the best in the world. Hence his omission from the side that toured the West Indies seemed to have little to do with playing ability. With the benefit of hindsight the selectors must have silently admitted their mistake. The 'quietly efficient' Krishnamurthy was competent behind the stumps but completely failed to impress with the bat; in 6 innings he managed a total of 33 runs, an average of 5.5. The end of the West Indies tour marked the end of Krishnamurthy's Test career and Farokh was selected for the next four series where he played in every match.

The success of the West Indies tour owed much to the arrival of a new cricketing star, Sunil Gavaskar. In 4 matches he scored as many centuries, making a total of 774 runs at an average of 154.8. This was the best Indian batting performance in their Test history and rivalled the achievements of Everton Weekes and Don Bradman. Farokh and Gavaskar were later to become opening partners as well as good friends:

36 Test centuries between them – only 34 from Sunil.

My mate Sunil Gavaskar made his name on that West Indies tour with his prolific scoring. I always called him 'the little master' because he was by far the best batsman India had ever produced. He had great concentration, tremendous determination and great skill, and when you combine these three qualities you have a truly great legend. His record of 34 Test centuries speaks for itself. I certainly enjoyed batting with Sunil and one of the most memorable occasions was when John Snow shoulder-charged him during the Lord's Test of our successful 1971 tour. I stroked the ball and called for a quick single. Sunil, who was at the non-striker's end, responded, but halfway down the pitch John Snow shouldered him to the ground and poor old Sunil went flying – bat and pads all over the place. I went up to Snow and said, 'Snowy, why don't you pick on someone your own size?' He had become so frustrated at his inability to claim our wickets which would have secured an England victory. Sunil became a slip fielder and that was partly my doing since to begin with Wadekar used to field in the slips but became distracted by my habit of chatting to the slip fielders and moved himself to a different position. Gavaskar took his place and we soon developed a good rapport having a chuckle and a joke between balls and between overs.

The India selectors effectively admitted their mistake in not selecting Farokh for the West Indies tour by immediately including him in the side to play a three-Test series against England during the summer of 1971. Krishnamurthy acted as Farokh's reserve and played in most of the county games while Farokh was engaged with Lancashire. The 1971 tour of England marked India's arrival as a major cricketing power, destroying for good the previous distinction between first and second division cricketing nations. To a certain extent this barrier had already been breached when India won their series in the West Indies, but the series against England, the home of cricket, demonstrated beyond doubt that the achievement of the previous winter was more than a flash in the pan. The tour of England consolidated India's position amongst the aristocracy of cricket.

The previous tour of England in 1967 had been a sustained disappointment both in the county matches and the Tests. This time India lost just once in 19 matches – in the county game against Essex. Farokh played in all 3 Tests and the county game against Glamorgan at Cardiff where he assisted India's victory by scoring 62 not out and 28. In the First Test, played at Lord's in July, Farokh's keenest memory concerns one of his most remarkably spectacular catches, which won the admiration of England's wicketkeeper, Alan Knott:

I'll never forget him catching John Edrich... off the bowling of the left-arm spinner Bishen Bedi. John got a thick edge, which saw the ball hit Farokh on the body and as it fell towards the ground he flicked it up into the air with his left foot (he's right footed too!) to take a truly unbelievable catch.

Farokh's recollections of this incident are substantially the same as those of Knott, though characteristically a little more colourful and entertaining:

This was the last ball of the day and Edrich was going great guns. Bedi made a quicker delivery and the ball pitched in the rough in the bowler's footmarks and took off. It clipped the shoulder of John Edrich's bat with the result that the ball went straight up and caught me on my left shoulder. Because of recent rain the ground was wet and skiddy and I was sprawled out on the ground when the ball came down. I just managed to flick it up with my left foot – a perfectly timed shot of which Bobby Charlton would have been proud – but as the ball came down again there were no fielders in the right position and it was impossible for me to take a catch so I kicked it up again, regained my balance and managed to finally catch the ball with a diving leap. John Edrich looked incredulous and muttered something unrepeatable as he began the walk back to the pavilion.

At the time of the Lord's Test match the Indian team were received at Buckingham Palace by the Queen. This occasion provided a difficult moment for the Indian team manager, Colonel Hemu Adhikari:

The royal reception was held in the evening. It was a cocktail party with plush red carpets, champagne and various eats. Now Colonel Adhikari had a passion for peanuts and he would flick them into his mouth from all directions. He grabbed not one but two handfuls at the very moment that the doors opened and Her Majesty the Queen was announced. As tour manager

Adhikari was expected to shake hands with the Queen first, but he was unable to respond to her outstretched hand because both his fists were clenched tight clasping peanuts. Fortunately for him there is a traditional form of greeting in India known as the namaste *whereby a slight bow is accompanied by palms pressed together in front of the chest or face. Adhikari had the presence of mind to adopt this pose but as he raised his arms peanuts trickled down his sleeves and I believe one or two became lodged in the Queen's shoe. The team were killing themselves laughing.*

The Lord's Test ended in a draw, a result which one commentator described as 'a cruel anti-climax'. After winning the toss England were dispatched for 304 with Farokh catching Boycott off the bowling of Abid Ali and Amiss and Illingworth off Bedi. India bettered England's first innings score of 304 by 9 runs. Although Farokh made a modest 28, it was the style of his batting which impressed the journalists. Writing in *The Guardian*, John Arlott expressed the view that 'Engineer is good for other batsmen'. He 'drew Viswanath out from beneath his bushel' and the pair 'emerged together from doubt to something near gaiety, the crowd reacting happily to Engineer's exuberance and determination to keep the game moving'. England were then bowled out for 191. Only Gavaskar with 53 and Farokh with 35 provided any serious batting resistance during India's second innings and according to John Arlott their stand of 66 in fifty minutes 'lifted the game to its highest level of entertainment'. Arlott called Farokh the 'bubbling extrovert of our cricket' who had 'altered the whole character of the match' with his attacking play. E.W. Swanton also noted how 'Engineer never needs long before he tries to shift the moral balance his way', and within ten minutes he had 'taken India completely out of the doldrums'. The omens were good for the rest of the series, for this was the first Lord's Test in which India had avoided defeat and was only the second Test played in England that India had achieved a first innings lead. Despite a second innings batting collapse brought about by a run chase in the face of a pessimistic weather forecast, India had revealed something of their new confidence and desire to win and had come closer to victory than on any previous occasion on English soil. Farokh's personal contribution clearly impressed Ken Barrington who, under the headline 'Action-Man Engineer is the Tops', wrote this appreciation in the *Daily Mail*:

Farokh Engineer, brilliant wicket-keeper and batsman extraordinary, was for me the man of a memorable Test. He is a player of spirit, action and adventure. When he heard a forecast of rain by mid-afternoon, he volunteered to bat No. 4, and go for the bowling. Skipper Wadekar wisely agreed, and Engineer with his knowledge of English conditions and weekly experience of Sunday League for Lancashire, very nearly won the Test for India. Perhaps his final act of charging down the wicket was too impetuous, but at least he brought the game to life, and England were more than thankful to see him go.

Meeting Mrs Gandhi (above) and the Queen (below).

Not only did Engineer set Lord's alight with his attack, he also caused a dressing-room flood. When he was running his bath-water, a roar from the crowd sent him rushing to the players' balcony. He became so absorbed in the drama he left the taps running. Water seeped under the doors, and cascaded from the roof before an attendant realised what was happening.

The Second Test played at Old Trafford also ended in a draw in which England clearly had the advantage. India were almost certainly saved by the Manchester rain when at 65 for 3 in their second innings and chasing a total of 419, the game was called off with no play possible on the final day. This meant that the Third Test scheduled to begin at The Oval on 19 August 1971 would decide the series. This was to prove the most significant match in India's thirty-nine-year Test cricket history. If India should lose they would also tarnish their claim to be taken seriously as the newcomers amongst the elite of cricketing nations. But should India win then the overseas victory against the West Indies would be fully validated and India would be acknowledged as potential world champions, having beaten the team that had recently humbled the mighty Australians.

For the third time in the series, England won the toss and Illingworth decided to bat. Under a clear blue sky the home side scored 355 all out with Farokh taking 2 catches which claimed the wickets of Edrich and Snow. The rain then set in and there was no play on the Friday. India's first innings began on the Saturday morning. John Woodcock commented on the 'desperately slow pitch', suggesting that 'Snow might as well have bowled a poached egg as a bouncer'. Nevertheless, the openers, Gavaskar and Mankad, both lost their wickets cheaply. Wadekar and Sardesai stabilised the innings in a partnership of 93 for the third wicket but then India soon found themselves at 125 for 5 after Viswanath had been bowled by Illingworth for a duck. This was the position when Farokh walked out to the crease. The state of play demanded a responsibly cautious innings as another 80 runs were required to save the follow-on and the situation was one to foster anxiety in some batsmen. In the words of E.W. Swanton, 'Engineer, for two vital hours, confronted England with just the right mixture of modified aggression'. After cutting his first ball for 2, Farokh, with his partner Solkar, put on another 12 runs before the tea interval. After the break, Illingworth continued at the Pavilion end and attempted to close the other with Hutton. John Arlott takes up the story:

> Engineer, however, played jauntily using his feet, driving with control and direction into the gaps of the field, until the follow-on figure was passed almost without remark.
>
> In the attempt to confine Engineer, Underwood bowled to him with a five-man onside field, four saving the one, and a deep square leg – sadly defensive tactics such as a spin-bowler of his quality should not need to employ on a

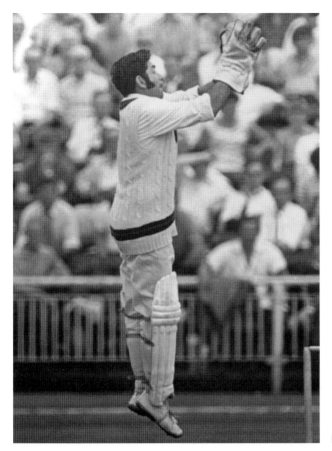

Bouncers – no problem.

turning pitch. It was England's only lapse of purpose. Engineer refused to be irked into recklessness, and he and Solkar were still together when Illingworth took the new ball three quarters of an hour from the end.

The partnership grew healthily, Engineer came gaily to his 50. Solkar driving and hooking spiritedly, seemed about to follow him when that arch change bowler D'Oliveira had him well caught at slip by Fletcher.

Engineer, of all people, made the highest score ever recorded in a Test in England without a boundary. Then in spite of the judgement behind his happy aggression, he destroyed himself in the last moment of the day. Unable to resist hooking a short ball from Snow, he skied a catch to mid-on and was walking out before it came down. There was affection as well as congratulation in the applause that welcomed him in.

Farokh's entertaining but controlled innings of 59 was the highest individual contribution towards India's total of 284, 71 runs short of England's first innings score. He had helped to steady the innings at a critical point when a batting collapse could easily have occurred, helped to avoid the follow-on, refreshed the crowds with his ebullient batting and secured one of the unlikeliest Test records in the history of the game. If this wasn't vintage Engineer, it was certainly a gritty and determined performance.

England's second innings witnessed one of the most remarkable bowling performances by Chandrasekhar, who finished with figures of 6 for 38. After only two and a half hours batting England were all out for 101, their lowest-ever score against India (England's previous lowest score against India was 134 at Lord's in 1936) and their lowest total in a home Test since they were bowled out for 52 at The Oval in 1952. Edrich, Fletcher and Snow all failed to score while Knott, Illingworth and Price all made less than 5 runs. This meant that India needed 173 runs to win with more than a day's play to accomplish the task. India were now on the threshold of their first Test match victory in England. The impossible dream must have seemed just that when Gavaskar was bowled lbw for his first duck in Test cricket. Mankad also lost his wicket before the end of the day's play, which ended with India at 76 for 2, only 96 runs behind the England total.

There was a carnival atmosphere at The Oval on the morning of Tuesday 24 August and a clear expectation amongst the sea of turbans and saris that this was to be India's day. After the match Illingworth joked that the Indians had the advantage of playing in front of their home crowd for every Indian tourist, businessman, waiter and schoolboy seemed to have passed through the turnstiles. It was the Hindu festival of Ganesh, the elephant-headed god, and an elephant had been borrowed from Chessington Zoo to parade around the

One of the best.

ground. But despite such a reassuring spectacle, India began the day badly, losing the wicket of their captain, Wadekar, to an unnecessary run out with the score still on 76. The backbone of the innings was then provided by Sardesai and Viswanath, who scored 48 – or half of the remaining deficit – at the painfully slow rate of one run every two minutes or so. Mihir Bose wrote that both batsmen gave the impression they were climbing Everest by the near-impregnable north col. Then, in the space of twenty minutes, India lost both the wickets of Sardesai and Solkar, the latter caught and bowled by Underwood on one. When Farokh strode out to the crease there were twenty minutes left before lunch and 39 runs needed for an Indian victory with 5 wickets gone.

No one was quite sure how he would respond to the tension. Farokh's instincts were always to attack and perhaps this was what a member of the crowd had in mind when he shouted, 'Remember you are playing for India, not for Lancashire'. The dilemma was posed by *The Guardian*: 'Engineer caused heartache and delight. Could so dashing a batsman survive such crushingly businesslike bowling and fielding?' The answer was 'yes', but not before he had aimed what E.W. Swanton termed 'a horrible whoosh' at his first ball and fortunately missed. Farokh then settled down and kept his head, providing a 'robust experienced front when it was most needed'. Punching the ball off the back foot, the 6th wicket ticked up another 12 precious runs before the lunch interval. At this point the crowd attached particular importance to the players' bill of fare and England's tactical shrewdness: 'Don't eat their fish and chips. Have a good plate of curry and rice.'

After lunch India began just 27 runs away from victory. By 2.40 p.m. they were 3 runs short of the total when Viswanath edged a catch to Knott. Abid Ali came in to bat and almost immediately risked his wicket with a rash stroke. Farokh walked up to his colleague to advise caution but the following ball was square-cut for 4, or rather, into the incoming tide of the pitch invasion. Campbell Page of *The Guardian* described the scene as 'like one of Eisenstein's crowd scenes'. Massed Indians leapt over the barriers and charged. Farokh and Abid Ali were swept towards the pavilion on the shoulders of the jubilant crowd while the umpires had gathered up the stumps and the English team had sprinted towards safety. This was England's first defeat by a national side under Illingworth's captaincy and brought to an end an unbeaten sequence of 26 Tests. After the match he told the crowd, 'The Indians have proved themselves to be a world-class side.' The celebrations continued in Calcutta where buntings and banners were hoisted to herald the Indian triumph. As the news swept the city, fans embraced each other and danced for joy in the streets. Mrs Gandhi cabled Wadekar: 'The country is thrilled to hear of your exciting victory.'

Farokh had played a key role in India's first series victory in England. According to Wisden, 'Engineer's performance behind the stumps was of the highest class' and his availability for the Test matches 'made the difference between defeat and victory'. Over 3 Tests he had taken 8 catches off some of the finest spin-bowling in the world (and it was approximately eighteen months since he had kept to the Indian spinners), provided entertainment at the crease and topped India's batting averages. Crucially, he had held his nerve at a critical point in the game and was in the spotlight at the very moment of his country's success. As he was lifted above the shoulders of the celebrating spectators he must have felt a sense of both national pride and personal achievement. He was a leading member of a side which, as judged by John Woodcock, had 'climbed the highest peaks in the cricketing world'. But because of commitments to Lancashire, Farokh was unable to accompany his team back to India where, despite the deepening political crisis over Bangladesh, Mrs Gandhi had the incoming plane diverted from Bombay to Delhi so that she could personally lead an official welcome to the cricketing heroes.

It was political issues in terms of the worsening relations between India and Pakistan that prevented India from receiving an English touring side during the winter of 1971-72. It was to be another year before India played host to England. In the meantime, a Rest of the World team was assembled, again under the captaincy of Sobers, to tour Australia between November 1971 and February 1972.

We touched down in Perth and in the airport lounge several gentlemen in suits came up to us who were members of the Perth Cricket Lovers' Society. They wanted to conduct some interviews and we had a chat with them. The next stop was Adelaide and again we were approached by a number of besuited gentlemen, members of the Adelaide Cricket Lovers' Society. Amongst them was a shortish fellow in a felt hat that one or two of us recognised as the greatest cricketer alive. Not so Tony Greig. He got off the plane with his holdall and clearly regarded this gentleman as one of the Cricket Lovers' Society. As if conferring an honour he asked him to hold his bag while he disappeared into the gents' to freshen up. Reappearing, he engaged his new acquaintance in conversation. 'Now then, do you have anything to do with Australian cricket?' 'Have you ever played the game?' And as the questions went on eliciting a succession of modest replies – 'Yes, I suppose so', 'You could say I've played a bit' – Sobers and I thought things were getting a bit serious and decided to put Greggy out of his misery. Sobers walked up to greet the Don, who had been playing along with the gag, and poor old Greggy's face was a picture of embarrassment – we never let him forget.

On this occasion Farokh was one of three Indian players selected for the tour alongside Gavaskar and Bedi. His selection was confirmation, if any was needed, as to his ranking as a world-class wicketkeeper. But Farokh continued to impress with the bat, scoring 104 against Queensland at Brisbane and 192 against Tasmania Combined on 27 and 28 December at Hobart, an occasion when Bob Taylor kept wicket. 192 was Farokh's highest score in first-class

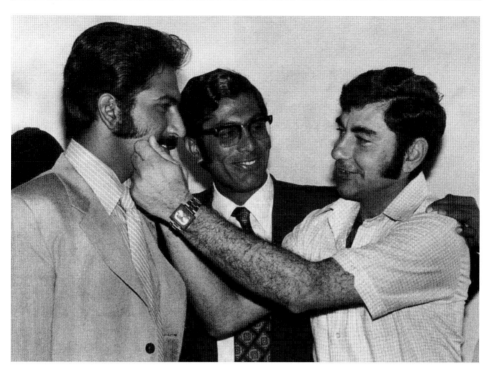

India-Pakistan rivalry?

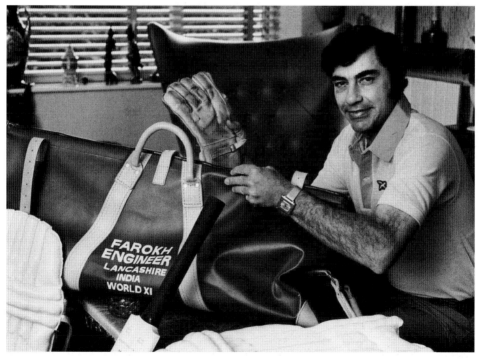

Off to Australia, World XI series, 1971-72.

Preparing for the World XI with Gavaskar in Sydney.

World XI team, tour of Australia 1971-72.

cricket and his innings, described by Ray Robinson as 'chanceless', included 17 fours off 60 overs before he was stumped by Cass off a flighted off-break. Playing under the leadership of Gary Sobers enabled Farokh to observe one of the greatest masters of the game at close quarters:

The very word 'great' you can associate with one man who was the most complete cricketer of all time – none other than Garfield St Auburn Sobers. A great man, a great player and a great friend – though it was never easy to get close to him and we are better friends now than in our playing days. He was as quick a fast bowler as anyone in the business and a great spinner (left-arm Chinaman) who could turn the ball viciously. Everyone knows about his batting, one of the sweetest hitters of the ball in the world, but he could also field in virtually any position – a marvellous slip fielder and an outstanding deep fielder. He was hard to fault, there was just nothing wrong with his cricket.

Farokh's next series against England during the winter of 1972-73 represented the high watermark of his Test career. As in the previous series against England, Farokh emerged top of the Indian batting averages. It was also in this home series that he made his Test career best of 121 in the final Test, so ensuring that India's 2-1 lead in the series was put beyond England's reach. Disappointingly, the England team was less than full strength, lacking the presence of Illingworth, Snow and Boycott, but Tony Lewis' side shocked the home nation by inflicting a 6-wicket defeat at the First Test in Delhi. After a number of team changes, India then won the Second Test at Calcutta by 28 runs with Farokh scoring 75 out of his side's first innings total of 210. For much of this match Wadekar was unwell and Farokh captained in his place. Mihir Bose wrote that 'it was noticeable what a difference his bright, engaging approach made'. India also won the Third Test at Madras, partly due to the return of Pataudi, and then drew the Fourth Test at Kanpur. When India went into the Fifth and final Test at the Brabourne Stadium, Bombay, they were ahead in the series and would clinch a series victory provided they could avoid defeat. This was the scene as Farokh and Gavaskar walked out to the crease on the morning of 6 February 1973.

Gavaskar was dismissed for 4, bowled by Old, when the score was on 25. Farokh was then joined by his captain, Wadekar. According to John Woodcock, writing in *The Times*, Farokh used his bat 'like a cutlass', taking on 'every bowler fast and slow alike', concluding that 'the spirit of his batsmanship, the effrontery of it, was wonderfully refreshing'. Robin Marlar of *The Sunday Times* claimed that by attacking, Farokh 'set the tone for the match' and in the style of a warrior he was soon 'giving the England faster bowlers the half-charge, smiting them as he went'. An unattributed article in *The Guardian* described Farokh's achievement as 'magnificent', asserting that he thereby 'dashed the theory that he has not the skill and application to succeed outside

one-day cricket'. Michael Melford of *The Daily Telegraph* produced a fuller assessment:

> Engineer's innings was a highly enjoyable piece of batting. He is always good value and... his driving, often executed on the walk, was something to remember... apart from three speculative hooks he played through the morning with a blend of enterprise and responsibility. In the hour after lunch Engineer, dancing down the pitch to Pocock, and playing some admirable straight drives, led an assault which brought 63 runs to him and his captain... Engineer hurled himself gaily at anything like a half volley or dabbed delicately at the short ball outside the off-stump... Before tea Engineer reached 100 out of 176 amid pandemonium as 50,000 ecstatic watchers waved and shouted behind their barricades. After tea he and Wadekar passed the previous second wicket record against England of 168, which remarkable record they set up themselves nearly six years ago at Headingley.

Farokh's 121 was scored in 280 minutes and included 11 fours. England were eventually set a first innings target of 448 after another century from

Opposite page: A study in concentration.

Right: On your bike.

Viswanath. They exceeded this total by 32 runs. In India's second innings Farokh and Gavaskar took the score to 102 for no loss at the end of the fourth day's play, ensuring, in the words of *The Observer*, that the final day would be an 'exercise in filling time'. That is exactly what happened and when India declared at 244 for 5, the match was effectively over. The draw confirmed India's series win. Farokh was presented with a silver cricket bat together with a motor scooter:

I was due to fly back to England the next day and was unable to take the scooter. Some chap out of the crowd made his way over to me claiming that he was one of my former classmates from Don Bosco High School. Now I can remember all my exact contemporaries from that time and I had certainly never seen this man's face before – maybe he was in the year above or below. Anyway we got talking and he seemed to be a pleasant enough fellow. After a while I asked him if he could ride a scooter and then if he had one of his own. He could ride but didn't have his own bike. So I said, 'See that scooter over there, it's yours.' He was dumbfounded. It must have seemed an incredibly generous gesture on my part but, in truth, I didn't know what to

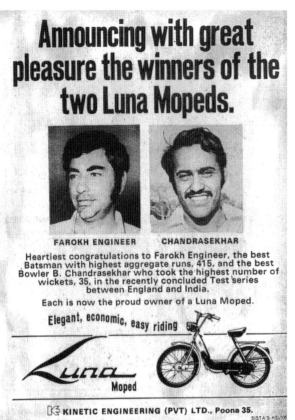

The series sponsors announce their awards. India v. England, 1972-73.

do with the prize machine. He was grinning from ear to ear, ran over to the scooter and wheeled it out of the ground as if he was the proudest man alive.

India's success against the West Indies and in the two series against England owed much to the quality of their spin bowling attack:

India had the four finest spinners in the world – Bishan Bedi, Erapalli Prasanna, Bhagwat Chandrashekhar and Srinivas Venkatraghavan (the last two were always known as Chandra and Venkat in England) – and to keep wicket to this famous quartet was a great experience.

Bedi was the perfect left-arm spinner with a wonderfully graceful action. He never got flustered and was capable of bamboozling the most skilful batsman with his seemingly endless bag of tricks. He was certainly not afraid of being hit and I always liked batting against him when he bowled for Northants because he gave a lot away to the ball. Bishan was a tremendous competitor and a great sportsman, the crowds loved him.

Prasanna was, in my opinion, the finest off-spinner India had produced. He had the most confusing variation of pace and would ensnare the best batsmen in the world. He didn't play as much Test cricket as he should, partly through taking time off to complete his engineering studies and partly through the inexplicable machinations of Indian cricket politics. But batsmen feared him and Pataudi always appreciated his true value.

Chandra suffered from polio as a child and this left him with a deformed right arm – it was literally an inch thick in places. But he was able to convert this misfortune into a tremendous cricketing asset. I had tremendous admiration for him. His wrist action was like a whip and he bowled leg-breaks, googlies and topspin at considerable speed. Indeed, he was sometimes the fastest bowler in the side. Batsmen found him incredibly difficult to read because he could turn the ball both ways, achieving considerable variation in bounce and pace. He wasn't much good as a batsman. In fact he is the only cricketer to have scored fewer runs in his Test career than the number of wickets he took. The Australians recognised this by presenting him with a bat with a hole in the middle on the 1977-78 tour. Of course, Chandra saw the funny side.

Venkat was not a regular member of the side during these years, mainly due to the availability of Prasanna. Nevertheless he was a highly accomplished off-spinner and achieved excellent figures during the West Indies tour of 1970-71. Of course he is now one of the most respected umpires on the international circuit.

The magic of the spin quartet failed to deliver for India's tour of England during the cold and wet first half of the summer of 1974. Everything had looked so promising with England's recent track record against New Zealand and the West Indies suggesting that India could probably continue their success story. But injury, division within the side and a change in the cricket laws whereby the number of on-side fielders was restricted to five, all compounded India's batting problems. Farokh was impeded by a pre-season ankle injury which clearly affected his keeping during the First Test at Old Trafford. He took 4 catches but was clearly off form. England won the match by 113 runs. During the Second Test played at Lord's, Chandra sustained a finger injury at an early stage in the England first innings and was unable to bowl again. England responded by scoring 629 with centuries from Amiss, Denness and Greig. India began well in their reply and Gavaskar and Farokh put on 131 for the first wicket. But with a total of only 302, of which Farokh scored 86, India were forced to follow on. The Monday play provided India's greatest Test humiliation. In 17 overs they were bowled out for their lowest Test innings score of 42 with only Solkar, who was not out for 18, scoring more than 5 runs. Farokh was lbw to Old for a duck, though he claimed he got an edge. England had won by an innings and 285 runs. The series was already lost and there was nothing to salvage except pride during the final Test at Edgbaston. For the first time in the series India won the toss and Wadekar decided to bat. Farokh was the highest scorer with 64 not out in India's total

Playing the fool, Old Trafford Test, 1974.

of 165. England declared their innings on 459 for 2 with Lancashire's David Lloyd making 214. India were then bowled out for 216 with Farokh scoring 33. This was only the third time in England that a side had won a Test match after losing just 2 wickets. India's failure was made complete by defeats in the two one-day games, though ironically they enjoyed relative success on the county circuit where for the first time on an English tour they remained undefeated. Commenting on Farokh's contribution to the series, Wisden stated that after the disappointments at Old Trafford, 'Engineer... lent weight to the batting with innings of substance and dash in each of the remaining encounters'. Apart from Naik, who played in just one Test, Farokh was top of the Indian batting averages. But he would be the first to admit that this had been a disastrous series for India after the achievements of the previous three years.

Farokh's final Test series took place at home against the West Indies. Pataudi had now replaced Wadekar as captain. Farokh's dismissal during India's first innings in the First Test was a clear piece of bad luck:

Andy Roberts was bowling and I on-drove the ball really hard, middled it, and Viv Richards turned round to avoid a possibly nasty accident. But the ball went straight towards him and lodged between his legs. Roberts shouted, 'don't move, don't move,' and he plucked the ball from between Viv's knees.

Applauding Solkar's brilliance.

It was a truly freak catch, yet minutes later Gavaskar was out in much the same way.

Misfortune struck again when Farokh was keeping wicket during the West Indies second innings; he was hit above the eye and had to retire injured. With Pataudi also off the field due to a dislocated finger that meant that India were down to nine men during their second innings. The West Indies won by 267 runs. The margin of defeat was even greater at the Second Test at Delhi where the West Indies won by an innings and 17 runs. Farokh's major contribution was a score of 75 in India's second innings. The tide then turned and India won 2 Tests in succession, the first time in their Test history that they had drawn level in a series after being 2-0 down. In 4 innings Farokh made a useful contribution with the bat, scoring a total of 127 runs. Behind the stumps he dispatched both Clive Lloyd and Viv Richards to the pavilion. All was square in readiness for the final Test at Wankhede Stadium, Bombay. After winning the toss the West Indies chose to bat and declared at 604 for 6. India replied with 406. The West Indies then declared their second innings at 205 for 3 and India were bowled out for 202 runs. The West Indies had won by 201. Farokh had hoped to end his Test career with a batting flourish. It was not to be:

Not very happy memories. In my final game I got a pair, the dreaded pair that happens to just about everyone – even Bradman has a pair to his credit. I was so keen and I was so disappointed when I got that pair because I was out to a very mediocre bowler called Julien who I used to hit all over the place when he played for Kent. In the first innings Viv Richards held a brilliant catch but in the second, the ball hit my inside edge, rolled onto my pads and trickled onto the stumps. I was really down and dejected after this experience and when I returned to England I felt my time was up.

That was the end of Farokh's first-class Test career. There was one more moment of glory, however, in the first World Cup, sponsored by Prudential Assurance, which was held in England in 1975. This was a limited-overs one-day competition and in the game against East Africa played on 11 June at Headingley, Farokh scored 54 not out, shared in a partnership of 123 not out with Gavaskar and was named man of the match. Farokh's international playing career had spanned thirteen years. During that time India had emerged from the shadows as a cricketing nation and Farokh had played a key role in the transformation from whipping boys to effective world champions. This was achieved partly through a number of sterling batting performances, partly through excellent displays of wicketkeeping and partly through the refusal to let adverse circumstances dampen his positive and cheerful outlook, an attribute which was often essential in order to sustain the morale of a team that was vulnerable to attacks of collective depression.

eleven

Life after Cricket

Farokh's professional cricketing career came to an end with the close of the 1976 summer season. The question of how to deal with retirement never arose, for he had already laid the foundations of a business career. If full-time opportunities had presented themselves in the media world Farokh would have been tempted to follow a different course, but his commentating contracts were too irregular to provide a livelihood. A life in the wings of cricket never appealed – there were simply too many ex-players attempting to drink from the same pot. It was only common sense that Farokh should make use of his training in sales and marketing and exploit the lessons he had learnt in the offices of Mercedes-Benz and Hawker Siddeley. So while many of his cricketing contemporaries became involved in the administration or coaching of cricket, Farokh confirmed his adopted Lancashire credentials by seeking his fortune in the textile trade. While his commercial activities began to flourish he also began a new life after the collapse of his first marriage by marrying Julie, a local girl from Blackburn, and starting a second family.

Full-time work was essential, for Farokh was far from being a wealthy man at the end of the 1976 cricket season:

Cricket was paying peanuts, though Clive Lloyd and I were said to be amongst the better paid overseas players in the country. We had a reasonably good living, we were often in the news and moving around in good company but we weren't really wealthy – certainly not in the Beckham class. I wanted to do something more responsible in life. I had played cricket at the highest level and now wanted a different challenge. After Hawker Siddeley I was offered a position in a textile firm. When I started off I knew about flying, cricket, sales and marketing but absolutely nothing about cloth! But my job involved selling the product and when you are selling you are basically selling yourself. The Managing Director of this firm was very keen to export to the Caribbean – he had tried to promote some business over there but with

Sharing a joke with Sobers and Lillee.

Married to Julie in Fiji.

Everything under control.

very little success and he thought I might do better since I was a familiar name over there. My first trip was to Jamaica. I was given a list of prices and information about the quality and designs of the various products. It certainly wasn't difficult securing interviews and being offered coffees, lunches and dinners. My name saw to that. But I was also able to set up a substantial level of sales and my boss was extremely impressed. I don't think the Jamaican wholesalers and retailers bought from me just because I was Farokh Engineer. After all, they were businessmen who needed to take their own cut. They weren't going to buy from me as an act of charity – and I wouldn't have wanted them to do so. I believed and I'm sure they believed that I was selling the right product at the right price and I quickly learnt what colours and designs were suitable for the Caribbean market. I spent four or five years doing well for the company but I eventually felt that I did not have enough opportunity to develop my own ideas and so I decided to start out on my own and be my own boss – I did not want to answer to anybody.

Over a period of time I developed and expanded my business, which prospered beyond my wildest expectations. Everything looked increasingly rosy until disaster struck: in 1991 my bank BCCI crashed and I lost a small fortune. I'm still smarting over it. In part, I blame the Bank of England

Earning a crust.

because they were meant to be a regulatory bank keeping check on all the other banks in the country to protect innocent people such as myself. We weren't engaged in any shady business, I was making an honest living. Neither was I getting any preferential service or interest rate from the bank. There were no special privileges. I was an ordinary customer. Up to that point, business had been going really well, the money was flowing in and I had had a few great years on my own. But then the Bank of England pulled the plug on BCCI and the bank collapsed – maybe it had been growing too fast too quickly and jealousies had developed in the banking community. There were all kinds of rumours. Many people had debit balances with the bank but I had substantial credit balances and overnight virtually the whole amount was lost.

My role in business was that of a middleman. I bought textile goods from manufacturers in Britain and Europe and then sold them on. At the peak of my success I used warehouses and would build up stocks so I could immediately satisfy the customers. There was obviously a risk involved, but if I could sell seven out of ten lines I would do well. As age takes its toll I take fewer risks and take samples over to my customers before placing the order. My list of buyers is now quite short but they are all friends and men I can trust. They know I have to earn a crust. Everything is based on trust and having a good name. I remember my father once saying to me, 'Son, it takes a long time to acquire a good reputation for yourself but you can lose it in an instant.' I've always heeded that advice and never knowingly betrayed anyone in business, though I've had it done to me a few times. I like to walk tall and sleep well at night.

Perhaps ninety per cent of my business is based in the Caribbean and Central and South America. Scandinavia and Europe accounts for the rest, with a little trade with Mauritius. Mauritius used to be a more important customer but the Chinese stepped in and they have fabulously competitive prices. It's destroying the work of many European exporters. When I go out to the Caribbean there is often an opportunity to look up old friends and spend some time with Wes Hall and Gary Sobers. The problem is that after a late night session that might go on until two or three o'clock in the morning you don't feel like getting up for an appointment at 8 a.m. – I now have to discipline myself so the business doesn't suffer. The only ex-cricketer I meet on my travels is Lance Gibbs who works for a shipping corporation based in Miami. We sometimes meet up in the Caribbean when he is arranging the shipping contracts. Otherwise this is a type of business where you never come across former cricketing colleagues.

It has been great fun. I love business – the hustle and bustle, the buying and selling, the negotiating with people. It gives me a sense of satisfaction and achievement. Not quite the same thing as hitting a six at the end of a game to clinch a victory but then it pays the bills. Being my own boss also suits me. You make your own perks and visit some wonderful destinations, though it can be a lonely life when you are travelling on your own. I've worked hard and tried to enjoy everything at the same time. My philosophy is that you can't take anything with you, so if the sun is shining it's off to the golf course.

Retirement from Lancashire and first-class cricket did not mean retirement from the game itself, and Farokh remained an active cricketer for many years:

In 1976 it was the end of my Test cricket and county cricket but still I had a lot of good years left in me – I enjoyed the game too much to lay down my bat and pads for good. I played for the MCC, the Lord's Taverners and for invitation World XIs and we toured all over the world. Invariably there would be an annual tour to Toronto and for some reason I was asked to captain a side that included John Edrich and quite a few West Indian players. Clive Lloyd came one year and we had some great tours, often to

On Concorde with Brian Johnston and Tim Rice.

Brands Hatch.

places one doesn't normally associate with cricket, such as Bermuda, Hong Kong and Bangkok. Tim Rice played for the Lord's Taverners and that was when we rubbed shoulders with stars like Mick Jagger, Keith Richards and Charlie Watts of the Rolling Stones. I've been on several tours with Tim Rice – we even made use of the same tailor in Hong Kong. I will never forget when Tim was bowling to a West Indian batsman in Charlotte in Carolina. The batsman kept whacking Tim in the mid-wicket region to a certain spot – the ball was hit a couple of times to the very same position. I went over to Tim and asked him to bowl a similar ball during his next over and added that I'd bet him my bottom dollar that the batsman would hit the ball right down my throat at mid-wicket. And sure enough that's what happened. Tim was amazed that I had predicted where the ball would go but these are the things you learn from cricket, from experience – you pick up the fact that the batsman has a swing in a certain direction. Mark Nicholas, who now works for Channel 4, was also on the tour to Carolina. I recall that instead of being paid a fee, the sponsors, who were a large department store, gave us $2,000 worth of shopping vouchers – our wives had an absolute field day.

One tour that was particularly memorable was to East Africa. Brian Close and his wife, Vivian, together with my wife, Julie, were on a Lord's Taverner's tour to Kenya. We were staying at the Mount Kenya Safari Club. On the day that we arrived we were having dinner in the open air with Brian and myself sitting on either side of the warden, who was not only a keen cricketer but an ex-SAS man. Suddenly some of his people came running towards us to say that they had just seen a pride of lions some hundred yards or so away. We were just finishing off our meal and drinking brandies so we decided to go and see the lions. We had a fantastic close-up view through the landrover window. It was beautiful to see the grand beasts in their natural habitat. We were so enthusiastic that the warden said that if we were not feeling too sleepy he would take us to a leopard-infested area and we would almost certainly see some more wildlife. As we drove along he told us how somewhere around the place we were presently driving across one of his vehicles had got stuck in a nasty hole only a few days before. Just as he said this we also hit a huge hole and the landrover was stuck. The more the driver accelerated the deeper we went and there was no way out but to leave the vehicle to seek help – we could have spent the night in the jungle and hoped to be rescued the following day but the ladies didn't fancy that as they all kept imagining that the silent leopards were watching our every move. The SAS man suggested that if one of us was to climb onto the roof and take control of the mounted searchlight he would run as far as he could in the beam of the light to fetch help. He suggested that everyone in the jeep should make as much noise as possible to scare away the leopards. I looked at Closey and said, 'you're the brave one, you took Charlie Griffiths and Wes Hall all over your body, you go up on the roof.' 'You must be f—ing joking,' he said and I replied that if I ever wrote a book I'd call him the biggest bloody

On safari.

coward around and that all the stories about him being hard as nails were untrue. There was no choice, I was the only other man and I had to go onto the roof with the searchlight and I was absolutely petrified. The wives started screaming to create a din and the SAS man jumped out of the jeep and ran into the distance. I followed him with the light until he disappeared and then dived back inside. After two or three hours we saw some lights. It was Fred Rumsey, the ex-Derbyshire player, together with a team of rescuers. We were towed out of the hole and then drove back to safety. But I'll never forget Brian Close, the brave one, celebrated for his battle scars but frightened of leopards. Don't get me wrong, he's a very good friend and we have been on quite a few tours together – a lovely character.

In addition to the foreign tours I played in the Lancashire League. I played for Tonge in the Bolton League and for Woodhouses, but this was mainly as a bowler – it made a change from wicketkeeping. It was at Woodhouses that I first came into contact with Mike Atherton and his father, Alan. When I first saw this kid coming on to bowl leg-spinners I little realised that here was a future captain of England and a prolific opening batsman. Lancashire League games took place at the weekends and we were playing with butchers, bakers, mechanics and all kinds of tradesmen. I remember one guy who ran a market stall would always arrive just minutes away from the start of the match and his pockets were stuffed full of notes. We used to joke that he didn't need a thigh pad – the pound notes would do just as well.

Above: Senior citizens at the
late Paul Getty's cricket ground.

Right: Nat Puri holds court at
Trent Bridge.

Farokh never lost contact with his old county club and still attends the reunion dinners meticulously arranged by Keith Hayhurst, one of the Lancashire committee members. He can always be found in the members' enclosure during an Old Trafford Test match, especially when India are in town.

Farokh admits that, much as he likes the ricocheting life of a sales executive, he would have loved to have had a permanent job as a commentator, but felt that the broadcasting world was one of cliques and favoured sons:

Soon after the end of my cricketing career I was given an opportunity in broadcasting and commentating – something that I very much enjoyed and always looked forward to. I was absolutely delighted to receive an invitation from Test Match Special *because I had always regarded the programme as a great institution. But almost from day one I sensed that the set-up was something of a closed shop, a private party, and hence I was never taken on as a regular member of the team. I was very disappointed because I felt that I was just as entertaining, industrious and knowledgeable about the game as most of the commentators around at that time. I'm not talking about the senior commentators such as Brian Johnston or Christopher Martin-Jenkins, who were quite brilliant, but the lesser mortals who might have played the odd Test match or two and then considered themselves experts. I did wonder whether I was excluded because my accent was wrong or because I liked to speak my mind; the BBC didn't appear to like colourful characters who might question the correctness of an umpiring decision or rock the boat in some way. Whatever the reason, it was clear that my face didn't fit. I think the BBC was too fond of restrained, grey characters. Certainly all the best commentators have gone over to the other channels.*

One of the most memorable and humorous moments on Test Match Special *was when I was commentating with Brian Johnston. Brian was one of the finest commentators I have worked with and we always used to engage in a fair amount of banter. On this occasion India were about to win the World Cup at Lord's. Brian turned to me and said, 'Farokhers, India are about to win the World Cup for the first time. Do you think Mrs Gandhi will declare a national holiday tomorrow?' Well, I replied in the same manner: 'Johners, you won't believe this but Mrs Gandhi is an avid* Test Match Special *listener and I have no doubt at all that she will declare a public holiday tomorrow.' We were jesting, having a good laugh in the commentary box. But within minutes there was a message received from Mrs Gandhi's office, which was relayed to us at Lord's telling us that the Indian Prime Minister had heard our comments and had indeed declared a public holiday for the following day. A few months later I was in India at a function in New Delhi. When Mrs Gandhi heard that I was there she called me over. 'You didn't half put me on the spot,' she said with a twinkle in her eye.*

Test Match Special with Brian Johnston and Christopher Martin-Jenkins.

If Farokh was unable to secure a permanent position on *Test Match Special* he nevertheless made a number of contributions to TV commentating. He has acted as anchorman for Star TV, based in Hong Kong, and also worked for both cable TV and Sky TV. In fact, at the time of writing, Farokh has just returned from a studio guesting contract with Sky Sports for the 2003 World Cup in South Africa:

Contrary to some predictions of failure, the competition was a great success. I watched every game, especially when India was involved. The only frustrations related to events off the field and I couldn't help feeling sorry for the organisers when faced with England's vacillating position over the game in Zimbabwe. When I visited South Africa before the tournament I had the privilege of being introduced to Nelson Mandela. When he heard that I was from England he asked me why England were being so indecisive about this match. I shrugged my shoulders, said I wasn't sure and asked his opinion. As he put his hand on my shoulder I was so in awe of the great man that I seemed to feel waves of electricity shoot down my spine. He replied in just a few words that England should play so as not to disrupt the tournament. I think the players felt let down by the British Government, who refused to accept responsibility for the decision. I find it hard to distinguish between Zimbabwe's presence at the Commonwealth Games in Manchester in 2002, Britain's continuing trade and financial dealings with Zimbabwe and the clear pressure on the cricketing authorities to pull out from the Zimbabwean game. Cricketing events should not form the focus for the conscience of a nation.

Another unfortunate off-the-field event related to the hysterical reaction of some people in India to news of India's poor performance in a qualifying match that followed fast on the heels of their disastrous New Zealand tour. Effigies of the players were burnt in the streets and stones thrown at the family homes in protest. Even some of the commentators, including ex-Test players, aggravated the situation with their inflammatory comments. I found the whole episode most distasteful and said so. I always believed that India are a very good young side who have done India proud.

In every good tournament the quality teams do well but there are also some upsets. The 2003 World Cup was no exception to this. Australia, the favourites, won in fine style at the expense of India in the finals but nobody would have predicted that Kenya would qualify for the Super Sixes at the expense of the West Indies, despite Lara's genius – of course the weather and England's non-performance in Zimbabwe both contributed to this outcome. Both England and Pakistan were at one point in an excellent position to beat Australia but Aussie grit pulled them through. Australia were magnificent and Gilchrist and Hayden are surely as devastating an opening partnership as any in the world today, almost on the same level as Sehwag and Tendulkar. Australia's edge over India was perhaps gained with their more experienced bowlers. Man for man the teams are very similar in strength but India's youngsters buckled under the intense pressure in the final. Nevertheless, India had a great tournament. Tendulkar proved yet again in the showcase of world cricket that no other batsman can touch him (even the Australians appreciated that he is in a class of his own) and there were also great bowling performances by Ashish Nehra who helped to destroy England's hopes of qualifying. Words of praise should be offered to the two youngsters, Yuvraj Singh and Mohammad Kaif, who performed well in all departments. I was also impressed by the improved captaincy of Ganguli – not forgetting his swashbuckling style of batting – and the ever rock-solid Dravid who provided the mainstay of the Indian batting together with an admirable display in the wicketkeeper's position which exceeded all expectations. Overall this was a great competition and a tremendous advertisement for the game.

Overall Farokh's relationship with the media has been a happy one. As a player he provided them with headlines, eye-catching photographs and insights into the state of play. As a commentator he provided expert opinion together with the occasional malapropism: 'If Gower had stopped that, it would have decapitated his hand,' or 'There must be something on Gooch's mind, and he wants to get it off his chest.'

At the Sky Sports studio with Darren Gough and Charles Colville.

Business affairs, cricket tours and commentating engagements have provided an exciting work and recreational dimension to Farokh's life but he would be the first to admit that it is his family that have given him most pleasure and happiness. As Farokh's mother's life was fading away she promised her son that she would return in spirit as his first child. Minnie, Farokh's oldest daughter, was born during the Lord's Test of June 1967. Indeed it was the Queen herself who broke the news to the expectant father:

I was with the rest of the team in the Lord's long room. Her Majesty the Queen was at the ground for introductions to the teams. Out of the corner of my eye I saw one of the Lord's officials hand over what looked like a telegram to Billy Griffith who was Secretary of the MCC. He passed on the paper to the Queen. I couldn't help wondering whether it had anything to do with me because I knew that my wife was about to give birth at any minute and was expecting some news. The next thing I knew was that the Queen had come up to me and said, 'Engineer,' (for some reason the royal family always addressed us by our surnames – I never felt this was right because I liked to be called 'Mr Engineer' or 'Farokh') 'I have some good

British captain of charity golf event.

news for you.' 'Is it a boy or a girl, Maam?' I said. 'What did you want?' she replied. 'A girl,' I said. 'Well, you have got one.' And that's how I received the news of Minnie's birth.

Minnie now assists her father with his business by managing a retail outlet in Sale, Manchester. She is also a qualified beautician and child nurse but Farokh is pleased to have at least one member of the family assisting his commercial activities and is extremely appreciative of her flair for interior designs. Tina, the second daughter, now lives in the United States where she works for an international company based in Miami. Farokh describes Tina as an extrovert with her father's personality, highly competitive and successful with a proficiency in both French and Spanish. Minnie and Tina are the offspring of Farokh's first marriage to Sherry, whom he met in Bombay during his early cricketing career. When this union sadly disintegrated during the 1970s Farokh met Julie, who is now the mother of Roxanne and Scarlett. The fateful first meeting with Julie took place at a beauty contest where one of Julie's friends was a contestant and Farokh one of the judges. When Farokh was introduced to Julie he asked her why she was not one of the contestants too. Julie took this question as an expression of interest. She was not wrong. They married in 1987. Farokh's sporting abilities have been passed down to his youngest daughter, Scarlett Bianca:

Four daughters: Minnie, Tina, Roxanne and Scarlett.

Little Scarlett is an extrovert. She's a bit like me, has my personality and more than believes in herself. I think she might make a name for herself in sports. I'd like her to, for the name of Engineer has to carry on. She plays netball and is a junior county player but she loves all ball games. Of course she wants to be a singer, a pop star – don't they all? I know she's proud of her father and she has told me, with tongue in cheek, that if she gets married she's going to keep the name Engineer.

Roxanne is more reflective and reserved:

Roxanne is more artistic than sporting. She's a very attractive and unassuming young lady – quite unlike her father! With her figure I think she's going to become a model, a top-class model. She certainly should be and thank God she has got her mother's looks! But I would not put pressure on any of my children to follow any particular career. I would like them to develop their own personalities and do well in their lives. Whatever they do they will have my full support.

All four of my daughters are very warm and affectionate, caring, loving, attractive and beautiful in every way. I'm extremely proud of them.

The Engineer household is a happy one: noisy, full of laughter and chattering with an easy and relaxed approach to life. Farokh presides over his domestic

Two right hookers.

kingdom like a benevolent despot, shouting orders, issuing demands and requests that invariably result in the speedy appearance of a willingly dutiful daughter; any excuse to share a few more moments of their busy father's time. This lordly style results, in part, from the fact Farokh is completely impractical and therefore totally dependent upon those he lives with: whenever a TV station seems unobtainable or an appliance fails to work, Julie is summoned from the nether regions of the house to carry out the repair or push the correct button. She admits that Farokh would buy a new video recorder or cassette player before he would learn how to change a plug or set a programmer. This failure to come to terms with the electronic and mechanical gadgetry of the modern world is shared by at least one of his daughters, for when Farokh once requested a bottle of beer for his guest, Roxanne appeared with the bottle together with a plastic potato peeler – the corkscrew was not to be found. Whereas many men fill their spare room, shed or garage with hand tools, work benches and power drills and sanders, Farokh's main recreation room provides space for a full-size billiard table presented to him by Steve Davis. Around the walls of what amounts to a cricketing museum are signed cricket bats, leather balls and photographs of Farokh with the rich and the famous – from leading sportsmen to popular entertainers and world statesmen. These mementoes are a fond reminder to Farokh that he was once a sportsman of rare distinction, one of India's stars who helped to change his country's cricketing destiny.

Anyone for snooker?

Yes, Prime Minister.

Left: Honorary Mancunians.

Below: Best of friends.

twelve

Reflections

Farokh Engineer played his first first-class cricket match in December 1958 and his last in September 1976. In the course of 46 Test matches he established himself as India's first-choice wicketkeeper and was publicly acknowledged as the best in the world when selected for the Rest of the World XIs in the early 1970s. His Test batting average of 31.08 was far superior to those of his immediate Indian wicketkeeping predecessors such as Tamhane (10.22) and Joshi (10.89) and far outdistanced two of his three principal rivals, Indrajitsinhji (8.5) and Krishnamurthy (5.5). Only Kunderan with an average of 32.7 was a serious challenger with the bat, and he was more of a fielder than a wicketkeeper. By October 2002, sixteen Indian batsmen have scored more runs for their country than Farokh and two of those above him in the rankings have lower averages; they are his wicketkeeping successor, S.M.H. Kirmani (27.04) and the all-rounder Kapil Dev (31.05). Three places below Farokh in an aggregate Test batting table is his former captain, Wadekar (31.07). Judged by contemporary international standards, Farokh played against a dozen wicketkeepers during his Test career: seven, including Hendriks, Jarman and Taber, had a batting average of less than 20, three (J.T. Murray, D.L. Murray and Wadsworth) an average between 20 and 30, and two had an average exceeding his own – I.L. Mendonca (40.5) who played only 2 Tests and Alan Knott (32.75) whose average was just 1.67 higher. But averages and statistics are anathema to Farokh, who quite rightfully claims that they tell the least interesting part of the story and can both exaggerate and diminish a cricketer's significance. Certainly they reveal nothing about the quality, style or importance of an innings or wicketkeeping performance. Nor do they provide any insight into the drama or entertainment value of a match. Since Farokh was, above all, an entertainer, he understandably prefers verbal assessments to cold and sometimes unforgiving rows and columns of statistics. Hence in this final assessment of Farokh Engineer, the cricketing cavalier, we will concentrate exclusively on what commentators and fellow players had to say and write about him.

A moment to remember.

There is a striking level of consistency in the assessments of Farokh's cricketing career: his wicketkeeping is universally applauded while his batting performances are usually seen as eccentric but entertaining. There is unanimous agreement that his overall contribution to the game was both positive and enhancing. Farokh was not an enigmatic or multi-faced character and what varies between the different accounts are the images and metaphors: the uninhibited nature of his wicketkeeping has been compared to that of a performing seal while the high leaps in the air to take a one-handed catch remind another writer of the action of a goalkeeper; his sometimes unorthodox style of batting was once described as 'an inspired mixture of golf, squash and hockey'. A valedictory article in the *Manchester Evening News* from October 1976 began with the words, 'A light will go out of county cricket next season when Farokh Engineer, Lancashire's Indian Test wicketkeeper, calls it a day.' One of Farokh's best-informed judges was John Kay, one of the most experienced cricket reporters in the north of England and cricketing correspondent of the *Manchester Evening News* for more than a generation. He was an almost unqualified admirer of Farokh's wicketkeeping skills, though a sterner critic of his batting:

> His wicket keeping is on a different plane to any Lancashire have had before. Duckworth was sound, highly skilled and often spectacular. Farrimond was the efficient and always reliable wicket keeper who could get runs in his own dour way. Both contributed much to Lancashire cricket, yet they could not make it

A moment to forget.

sparkle to the extent Engineer has done. The Indian freely admits to being a showman. He likes to do everything the spectacular way. Yet he contrives to make it look not only safe but frequently easy. His uncanny anticipation and reading of a batsman's mind and a bowler's intentions enables him to be in the right place at the right time, and many a top-class batsman has left the crease completely bewildered at being caught behind the wicket off what he considered a well-played and ideally placed leg glance. There are times, in fact, when Engineer touches the heights of genius – and occasions, especially with the bat, when he infuriates by a lack of patience and understanding of the needs of the moment. Yet it cannot be denied or even doubted he is very much an entertainer as well as a cricketer. He has brought a touch of Indian magic to the Lancashire scene and slotted into the scheme of things so well that he has broken down all barriers and become one of the boys in every possible way.

(John Kay, *A History of County Cricket, Lancashire*, 1972)

John Marshall, author of books on Lord's, Headingley and Old Trafford, refers to both Buddy Oldfield, the Lancashire team coach, and Lancashire's chairman, Cedric Rhoades, as holding the view that Farokh 'is the finest wicket-keeper in the world'. Rhoades also gave considerable credit to Farokh for the 'happy and successful' state of affairs at Lancashire in the early 1970s and regarded him as 'One of the greatest chaps to have in the dressing room or anywhere else'. Marshall was glowing in his praise for the combined contribution of Engineer and Clive Lloyd, who must forever rank among the great Lancashire cricketers in every sense, combining boundless enthusiasm and unfailing courtesy with consummate skill and artistry. Certainly they have contributed handsomely to the cohesion, the mutual esteem, which have made contemporary Lancashire the most complete team in the county's history.

(John Marshall, Old Trafford, 1971)

Brian Bearshaw who wrote the official history of Lancashire County Cricket Club published in 1990 described Farokh as 'not only a brilliant wicket-keeper but a dashing batsman who was the bedrock of a side which was to be recognized as one of the best fielding teams the game has seen'. Farokh's impact on Lancashire's fielding performance was also appreciated by his former captain, Jack Bond:

> Farokh Engineer started Lancashire on the way back in 1968 and a lot of the praise about our fielding in those following years was due to the example this man set. He's so lively in the field he makes poor returns look good and lifts everybody's game.

(Manchester Evening News, 30 October 1976)

In 1984 Gerald Hodcroft, a long-standing member of the Lancashire club, privately published <i>My Own Red Roses</i>, a series of twenty-five pen portraits of famous Lancashire players from the days of Hornby to Lloyd. Hodcroft's vignette of Farokh colourfully illustrates both the strengths and weaknesses of his cricket:

> He was essentially a swashbuckler, a Parsee pirate, a pirate whose flashing cutlass was a bat. His swashbuckling made him vulnerable to almost any bowler in cricket who could turn an arm over, but on the other hand the best in the game were banged against the sightscreen or lifted into the tea-tent when he was at his most destructive… He could be (and often was) out to the most outrageous, unorthodox strokes, yet strode cheerfully from the wicket in the sure knowledge that there was always another day.
>
> When keeping wicket he seemed always on the move, and there was usually, when the ball had passed the bat and was in his gloves, a final flourish with the ball held against a stump, a warning to the batsman that he was hawk-eyed, vigilant, ready for a stumping, should the back foot be lifted the merest fraction of an inch…
>
> On and off the field he was a 'character' and a credit to the game. He was forever chattering to whoever might listen, and he chatted alike to those who might not. As a Parsee he must have known all about the Towers of Silence, but silence was never part of his make-up. There was always something to be cheerful about and he was ever eager to share his cheer with others.

A laugh with Peter Reid and Gary Lineker.

Assessments of Farokh's performances on the international stage of cricket stress the same skills and qualities that he made available to Lancashire. *The Hindu* (18 August 2002) described him as 'exuberantly gifted' and claimed that he 'ennobled and enriched' the Indian Test sides in which he played. One of the most extended appreciations of his wicketkeeping talents has been provided by the Sri Lankan bowler, Gamini Perera:

> There was every reason to rank Engineer as one of the premier wicket-keepers. Day in, day out, he would do the most thankless job in wicket-keeping to spinners, with remarkable ability and enthusiasm. Squatting to spinners on wickets of uneven bounce can be unnerving to the best of wicket-keepers and many develop a hang-dog look about them. Scowling and fuming they seem to be resigned to the cruelty of their fate.
>
> But Engineer was of a different genre altogether. He actually relished the difficulty of keeping to the wiles of Prasanna, the curvature of Bedi and the accuracy of Venkataraghavan…
>
> The manner in which he took the medium paced spin of unorthodox Chandrasekhar down the leg-side and whipped off the bails amazed all as it amazed the batsman. Earlier in his career, he was quite at home to Durani, Umrigar, Borde and Nadkarni. Athletic and acrobatic, he was a top-class performer…

Engineer was a wicket-keeper extraordinary. A man who brought the low profile wicket-keeper into public focus. In the 1940s, and 50s, India had the perky Sen, the steady Tamhane, the safe Joshi and the boisterous Kunderan, but none really had the performer's appeal to draw attention. When Engineer took the field against Dexter's England side in 1961/62, one could instantly gauge that there was a man with a difference. The gait, the manner, the approach suggested that at last India had found a man who had the cavalier flair for adventure, the spirit to go into the realms of the unknown.

In a Test career which spanned from 1961 to 1976, Engineer was all youth and exuberance. Never for a moment did he appear sullen or listless, dull or withdrawn. Bubbling with excitement and confident of his ability, he altered the whole ethos of wicket-keeping.

Apart from England's Godfrey Evans, no other wicket keeper did his job with such gusto as Engineer. Being an extrovert, Farokh thankfully saw no reason to change his natural inclinations. He distanced himself from the concept that wicket-keepers should be grim and shorn of flamboyance. He was the person who gave wicket-keepers an identity that they be throaty and thrilling; full of flair and glamour; that they should be the pivot of exuberance and inspiration on the field.

(The Island, 2 June 2002)

The more formal and established cricketing reviewers are briefer but equally complimentary. H. Natarajan in his 'Wisden overview' described Farokh as 'A flamboyant batsman and an agile wicketkeeper… one of the best of his trade', while Christopher Martin-Jenkins provided this summary:

One of the best wicket-keepers India has produced… a cricketer of immense character. Everything he did on a cricket field was alert and keen. He was an unorthodox right-handed batsman who either opened or went in between six and nine and his whole approach was brisk, confident and aggressive. A good square-cutter and strong driver, his great strength was on the leg-side: he could 'work' practically any delivery to mid-wicket. As a wicket-keeper he was brash and brilliant, the enthusiastic pivot of all that went on in the field. He could reach the widest leg-glances with an acrobatic dive and have the bails off in an instant if the batsman's back foot was raised. He clearly revelled in taking and then disposing of the ball in the slickest and most stylish manner possible.

(C. Martin-Jenkins, *Complete Who's Who of Test Cricketers,* 1980)

Farokh's career and cricketing qualities can be charted also through the headlines he attracted many of which read like captions from a *Boys Own* magazine – heroic, daring and uplifting: 'Engineer To The Rescue', 'Engineer Strikes Out On His Own', 'Engineer Defies Doctor', 'Fearless Farokh Hors De Combat', 'Brilliant Engineer Takes Flying Catch', 'Farokh Scorns Safety Tactics', 'Engineer Lifts Gloom', 'Engineer Makes Sussex Suffer', 'Six Victims For

Hitting the headlines.

The authors and two treasured trophies – a pure silver cricket bat and the golden glove.

Engineer', 'Engineer Steadies Wilting Indians', 'Engineer Again Lashes Out', 'Engineer's Wicket Is 'Wasted''.

There can be no doubt that Farokh Engineer was a major force in Indian cricket, a man who almost single-handedly revolutionised the role of wicketkeeper and converted the plot of green behind the stumps into a staging ground for his acrobatic leaps, warcry appeals and theatrical flourishes with the ball and gloves. While playing for Lancashire the position of first slip was referred to as 'Butlins', for Farokh ensured with his sideways dives that the fielder was surplus to requirements. But if his style of wicketkeeping was borrowed from the circus and trapeze artist, it was none the less effective, and although the convention of cricketing appreciation is often eulogistic, the words 'brilliant', 'magnificent' and 'dazzling' are consistently used to encapsulate his talent. Perhaps it was precisely because of his unassailable position as both India's and Lancashire's first-choice keeper that he felt he had the licence to indulge his instincts with the bat. Here he could wreak havoc and despair amongst the opposition or succumb to impatience or impetuosity. On well-documented occasions he played with restraint and discipline but this was not his natural game. Game is perhaps the key word to Farokh's approach to cricket, because he saw it as just that. He could never have empathised with Bill Shankly's comment about football that it was more serious than a life or death affair. To Farokh a game was a contest played in good spirit with ever an eye for the entertainment of the crowd; only the most mean-minded of spectators wanted to watch a slow and painstaking match of attrition and he saw it as the responsibility of the players both to enjoy themselves and communicate that enjoyment around the ground. Although highly competitive, he was never obsessed with winning, for that led to tactics and modes of play that represented the very opposite of what he regarded as sportsmanship. Farokh was a gentleman player, a cricketing romantic with the sporting values of the medieval knight – courteous, fair-minded and honourable, yet courageous and steadfast in the face of danger. For that reason he will always occupy a fond niche in the memory of true cricket lovers.

Farokh Engineer's Dream Team for India

The following team is drawn from those cricketers I have seen or had the privilege to play with. Inevitably this excludes some of the great players of the late nineteenth and early twentieth centuries. Some of the players are obvious, automatic selections and their inclusion could hardly be a matter of controversy with any selector. Others are less obvious and I have had to exercise my personal preference. Sometimes the reason for including one player and excluding another has been wafer thin and I am conscious that many fine players – Prasanna, Bedi, Gupte, Dravid, to name but a few – have unfortunately been excluded. India has produced many talented cricketers over the last half-century or so and this is my list of favourites. With the exception of the last entry, the order is alphabetical.

Bhagwat Chandrasekhar

Chandra would surely be an automatic selection in anyone's Dream Team. Wisden nominated his 6 for 38 against England at The Oval in 1971 as the best bowling performance of the century and few could argue with that. He was the principal factor in India's first series win in England in 1971 and he also helped his country to their first Test win in Australia in 1978, taking 12 for 104 at Melbourne. Viv Richards considered him the most difficult bowler he faced and Chandra remains India's biggest matchwinner overseas with 42 wickets in 5 Tests. Turning adversity into fortune, his withered right arm provided the instrument for what many fine batsmen regarded as unplayable and unpredictable deliveries. Chandra was a feared and deadly weapon in India's bowling attack.

Kapil Dev

This great all-rounder would surely be an automatic selection in anybody's Indian team of greats. Kapil was a natural athlete who could have excelled at any sport – in recent years he has demonstrated his proficiency in golf. He remains the only Test cricketer to have scored more than 5,000 runs and taken 400 wickets. In 2002 Wisden named Kapil their Indian cricketer of the century and few could argue with this decision. Kapil had the ability to turn a game with his captaincy, bowling or batting. Two examples always come to mind: when he hit 4 consecutive sixes off Eddie Hemmings to avoid the follow-on in a Test against England in 1990 and when he came in to bat against Zimbabwe during the 1983 World Cup when India were 17 for 5; 60 overs later he had scored 175 and taken his country to 266 – I was commentating for *Test Match Special* during this feat. India won the World Cup in that year under Kapil's captaincy. Kapil began his Test career in 1978 so we never overlapped as Test players but I remember enjoying his performances as a commentator and spectator. In 2002 we were co-commentators and studio guests for the ICC Trophy held in Sri Lanka. He is now a successful businessman.

Sunil Gavaskar

Another automatic selection. Indeed, anyone who excluded Sunil would rightfully be regarded as quite mad, for he was the greatest Indian cricketer of his generation. With more than 10,000 Test runs and a record 34 centuries he was the complete batsman with a near unbreachable defence together with a glittering array of scoring strokes. I have never witnessed a batsman with such concentration, flair and technique. Sunil was the ultimate in cricketing professionalism: always responsible, cool-headed and dedicated to the task ahead. In addition to his batting he was an excellent slip fielder and was the first Indian, excluding wicketkeepers, to take more than 100 catches. But although Sunil was capable of great feats of concentration, this was never at the expense of his youthful spirits and we always exchanged wisecracks on and off the field – and continue to do so whenever we meet.

Vijay Manjrekar

Vijay was a gutsy, courageous player with a fine technique and oodles of ability – quite a rare combination amongst Indian cricketers of the 1950s and early 1960s. We played together at Test level for about four years until 'Tatt', as he was known, was dropped after scoring a century against New Zealand in February 1965. His captain wanted him to remain in the team but the selectors, in their wisdom, knew best. I witnessed his highest score of 189 made against England at Delhi in 1961-62 but his most remarkable Test achievement came before my time: a century scored in his first Test in England at Headingley in June 1952, a series when India were gunned off the field by the raw firepower of Fred Trueman. Like Gavaskar, Tendulkar and many other great batsmen, Manjrekar was short but a marvellous player of fast bowling and a great hooker of the ball. He could also bowl off-spin and even kept wicket on a number of occasions – his Test record includes 2 stumpings. In the Ranji Trophy he represented no less than six sides. Vijay Manjrekar was simply the best Indian batsman of his time, as a number of his contemporaries such as Gupte and Prasanna have agreed. Fitness became an increasing problem during the latter stages of his career and sadly he died relatively young in his early fifties.

Vinoo Mankad

Vinoo was one of the great Indian all rounders. Perhaps he would have achieved more recognition if India had won more Tests during his career – he was only on the winning side on 5 out of the 44 occasions. When Vinoo began his first-class career I wasn't even thought of and his last Test for India was played in 1959. This was a player I watched, heard about and admired. We also played together for the CCI in the late 1950s – I had the privilege to keep wicket to his bowling and join with him as the club's opening batsmen. He was always generous with his coaching tips: I had a tendency of moving my right foot further to the right, a sign of overconfidence, when facing bowlers; on one occasion in the nets he helped me to correct this error by tying a rope around my leg and attaching it to a stake. Some of his feats were legendary, such as when he scored 72 and 184 at Lord's in 1952 in addition to bowling 97 overs and taking 5 for 231 – this has been described as the greatest ever personal performance in a Test by a member of the losing side. I also remember following his opening stand of 413 with Pankaj Roy made against New Zealand at Madras in January 1956 – this was a series in which Vinoo scored 2 double centuries and ended up with an average of 105. He was also a great left-arm spinner of the Bedi class. As a batsman, Vinoo's qualities were great concentration and a strong defence, a great asset to any team – I believe he batted at all 11 positions in Test cricket. He too was a doctor's son.

Dattu Phadkar

Dattu was another extremely impressive all-rounder: an aggressive and determined middle-order batsman and an accurate medium-pace bowler who could swing the ball both ways. His heyday was during the decade immediately before I came on the Test scene. He was extremely good looking and all the girls used to fall in love with him. As a player, the best example of his talents at Test level must have been in the Third Test between India and England at Calcutta in 1951-52 when, batting at number 6, he scored 115 and took 4 wickets. Dattu captained Bombay in the Ranji Trophy and after his cricketing career was over went on to become a selector.

Harbhajan Singh

Harbhajan, or 'The Turbanator' as he is often known, is the youngest member of my dream team. Indeed, at just twenty-two, Harbhajan is easily young enough to be my son, if not my grandson! As I write he is still performing excellent work for his country and in October 2002 gained his tenth 5-wicket haul. 'The Turbanator' earned his name through his sometimes devastatingly effective off-spin bowling. With a whiplash action he can vary his length and pace, extract a good bounce and turn the ball both ways. These talents, combined with his intense competitiveness, self belief and passion for the game (sometimes mistaken for arrogance), enabled him to take 32 wickets against the Australians in a 3-Test series in 2001 – no other Indian player took more than 3. In the Second Test played at Kolkata, he took a hat-trick in the first innings dismissing Ponting, Gilchrist and Shane Warne in successive deliveries. Harbhajan is a committed and hardworking player with surely a great future ahead of him in Test cricket. I'm sure he will add significantly to his present tally of 144 Test wickets – not to mention a couple of fifties with the bat. I was delighted to add my unqualified support when Lancashire signed him on for the 2003 season.

Sachin Tendulkar

The only Indian cricketer to seriously rival Gavaskar's many talents as a batsman. Sachin may even break Sunil's records, for he has already accumulated nearly 9,000 runs and 31 Test centuries. Tendulkar is undoubtedly a great player, one of the best I have seen – mentally tough yet an elegant stroke player, a great entertainer and a supremely intelligent cricketer. These qualities have made him one of the most popular Indian cricketers of all time. I remember receiving him at my house on the eve of the Second Test at Old Trafford in 1990. Both teams were there along with all the commentators – Brian Johnston, Trevor Bailey and Freddie Trueman. Julie and I had organised a barbecue in the garden. A few days later Sachin scored 160 in the second innings to save the game; this was his first Test century. Perhaps the greatest compliment paid to Tendulkar was by Sir Don Bradman who cited him as the player most similar to himself in terms of batting technique. He is surely the best batsman in the world today.

Pahlan Umrigar

'Polly' would be my choice for the dream team's captain. Before Gavaskar he held the record for most Tests, most runs and most hundreds by an Indian player. One of his most memorable achievements was his 130 not out against England in 1951-52 which helped India to their first Test victory. But Polly would be my captain not because of his dependable batting, accurate off-spin bowling or brilliant fielding or even because he was a fellow Parsee or my boyhood hero. Polly would be my captain because I rated him the finest captain I served under. He had a commanding presence, an excellent sense of humour and was a shrewd tactician of the game. He could inspire his teammates but was not afraid to point out mistakes or examples of selfish or foolish play. It is a credit to his sound judgement that he later became a national selector and team manager.

Dilip Vengsarkar

At his best Dilip was one of the finest batsmen in the world. He was the first to score 3 successive hundreds against England at Lord's and in three seasons, 1986-88, scored 8 hundreds in 16 Tests. His best period was from the late 1970s to the late 1980s. Dilip was a tall and elegant stroke-player, a superb player of the drive and a courageous hooker. He belongs to that select club of Indian batsmen with a Test batting average of above 40 and in 1987 was named as Wisden Cricketer of the Year. Dilip led his country in 10 Tests and now runs a very successful cricket academy in Bombay

Farokh Engineer

What can I say? To justify my selection would be an invidious matter but then to leave myself out would imply a lack of confidence – I have rarely been accused of that. Hopefully what has been written on the pages in the main body of this book explains why I consider myself a serious contender for the position of India's wicketkeeper in this Dream Team.

Farokh Engineer
December 2003

Index

If you are interested in purchasing
other books published by Tempus, or in case you have
difficulty finding any Tempus books in your local bookshop,
you can also place orders directly through our website

www.tempus-publishing.com

or from

BOOKPOST
Freepost, PO Box 29,
Douglas, Isle of Man
IM99 1BQ
Tel 01624 836000
email bookshop@enterprise.net